China and East Asian Economic Integration

EAI Series on East Asia ISSN: 2529-718X

Series Editors: WANG Gungwu
(East Asian Institute, National University of Singapore)
ZHENG Yongnian
(East Asian Institute, National University of Singapore)

About the Series

EAI Series on East Asia was initiated by the East Asian Institute (EAI) (http://www.eai.nus.edu.sg). EAI was set up in April 1997 as an autonomous research organisation under a statute of the National University of Singapore. The analyses in this series are by scholars who have spent years researching on their areas of interest in East Asia, primarily, China, Japan and South Korea, and in the realms of politics, economy, society and international relations.

Published:

China and East Asian Economic Integration
    edited by Sarah Y TONG and KONG Tuan Yuen

Suzhou Industrial Park: Achievements, Challenges and Prospects
    by John WONG and LYE Liang Fook

Chinese Society in the Xi Jinping Era
    edited by ZHAO Litao and QI Dongtao

China's Economic Modernisation and Structural Changes:
Essays in Honour of John Wong
    edited by ZHENG Yongnian and Sarah Y TONG

Politics, Culture and Identities in East Asia: Integration and Division
    edited by LAM Peng Er and LIM Tai Wei

China's Development: Social Investment and Challenges
    by ZHAO Litao

China's Economy in Transformation under the New Normal
    edited by Sarah Y TONG and WAN Jing

*The complete list of the published volumes in the series can also be found at
https://www.worldscientific.com/series/eaisea

EAI Series on
East Asia

China and East Asian Economic Integration

Editors

Sarah Y TONG
East Asian Institute
National University of Singapore
Singapore

KONG Tuan Yuen
East Asian Institute
National University of Singapore
Singapore

NEW JERSEY · LONDON · SINGAPORE · BEIJING · SHANGHAI · HONG KONG · TAIPEI · CHENNAI · TOKYO

Published by

World Scientific Publishing Co. Pte. Ltd.
5 Toh Tuck Link, Singapore 596224
USA office: 27 Warren Street, Suite 401-402, Hackensack, NJ 07601
UK office: 57 Shelton Street, Covent Garden, London WC2H 9HE

Library of Congress Cataloging-in-Publication Data
Names: Tong, Sarah Y. (Sarah Yueting), editor. | Kong, Tuan Yuen, editor.
Title: China and East Asian economic integration / editors,
   Sarah Y. Tong, East Asia Institute, National University of Singapore, Singapore,
   Kong Tuan Yuen, East Asia Institute, National University of Singapore, Singapore.
Description: New Jersey : World Scientific, [2020] | Series: EAI series on East Asia, 2529-718X |
   Includes bibliographical references and index.
Identifiers: LCCN 2019057678 | ISBN 9789811200311 (hardcover)
Subjects: LCSH: China--Foreign economic relations--East Asia. | East Asia--Foreign
   economic relations--China. | East Asia--Economic integration.
Classification: LCC HF1604.Z4 E1824 2020 | DDC 337.1/5--dc23
LC record available at https://lccn.loc.gov/2019057678

British Library Cataloguing-in-Publication Data
A catalogue record for this book is available from the British Library.

Copyright © 2020 by World Scientific Publishing Co. Pte. Ltd.

All rights reserved. This book, or parts thereof, may not be reproduced in any form or by any means, electronic or mechanical, including photocopying, recording or any information storage and retrieval system now known or to be invented, without written permission from the publisher.

For photocopying of material in this volume, please pay a copying fee through the Copyright Clearance Center, Inc., 222 Rosewood Drive, Danvers, MA 01923, USA. In this case permission to photocopy is not required from the publisher.

For any available supplementary material, please visit
https://www.worldscientific.com/worldscibooks/10.1142/11279#t=suppl

Desk Editor: Lixi Dong

Typeset by Stallion Press
Email: enquiries@stallionpress.com

Printed in Singapore

Contents

About the Editors and Contributors		vii
Introduction *Sarah Y TONG and KONG Tuan Yuen*		1
Chapter 1	China and East Asia Production Network *LÜ Yue and Sarah Y TONG*	7
Chapter 2	The Internationalisation of China's Renminbi *WAN Jing*	33
Chapter 3	The Internationalisation of Chinese Enterprises *CHEN Chien-Hsun*	51
Chapter 4	Cross-Strait Economic Relations: Taiwan's Perspective *CHIANG Min-Hua*	67
Chapter 5	CEPA and Mainland-Hong Kong's Economic Relations *ZHANG Yang*	85
Chapter 6	China–ASEAN Economic Relations Remain Resilient Despite Rising Challenges *Sarah Y TONG and KONG Tuan Yuen*	103

Chapter 7	Ever-Bonding Sino–Korean Economic Relationship but Questionable Contribution to Regional Integration *CHOO Jaewoo*	119
Chapter 8	China and Japan: Great Economic Integration without a Bilateral Free Trade Agreement *XING Yuqing*	133
Chapter 9	The Political Economy of East Asia Economic Integration *John WONG & KONG Tuan Yuen*	151
Index		167

About the Editors and Contributors

Sarah Y TONG is Senior Research Fellow at the East Asian Institute (EAI), National University of Singapore. She obtained her PhD in Economics from the University of California at San Diego, and had held academic positions at the University of Hong Kong and National University of Singapore. Her research interests concentrate on the recent development and transformation of the Chinese economy. Her work appeared in journals such as *Journal of International Economics, Global Economic Review, China: An International Journal, Review of Development Economics, China and the World Economy, Comparative Economic Studies* and *China Economic Review*. In addition to contributing essays to numerous books on contemporary China, she edited and co-edited several books including *China's Economic Transformation under the New Normal* (World Scientific, 2017); *China's Great Urbanization* (Routledge, 2017); *China's Evolving Industrial Policy* (Routledge, 2014); *Trade, Investment and Economic Integration* (World Scientific, 2014); and *China and Global Economic Crisis* (World Scientific, 2010).

John WONG was a Professorial Fellow and academic adviser of EAI, National University of Singapore and former research director of EAI, and director of the Institute of East Asian Political Economy (IEAPE). He taught Economics at the University of Hong Kong during the 1966–1970 period and at the National University of Singapore from 1971 to 1990. He was a short-term academic visitor at the Fairbank

Centre of Harvard University, Economic Growth Centre of Yale University, St Antony College of Oxford University and Economics Department of Stanford University. He had held the ASEAN Chair at the University of Toronto.

Professor Wong had written/edited 40 books, and published over 400 articles and papers on China, and development in East Asia and ASEAN. His first book was *Land Reform in the People's Republic of China* (New York, Praeger, 1973) and his most recent book was *Zhu Rongji and China's Economic Take-Off* (London, Imperial College Press, 2016). He had also written numerous policy-related reports on the development in China for the Singapore government. He received his PhD from the University of London.

Professor Wong passed away in June 2018. For over three decades, Professor Wong had followed and provided insightful analyses on the remarkable transformation of China's economy.

KONG Tuan Yuen is a Visiting Research Fellow at the EAI, National University of Singapore. He received his PhD in Industrial Economics from the National Central University, Taiwan. His postdoctoral fellowship at the Research Centre for Taiwan Economic Development provided him with the opportunities to undertake Taiwan's economic research projects. He had also contributed actively to the Center of Southeast Asian Studies in Taiwan that holds the largest research community in Southeast Asia. He also had corporate experience in business management, financial and planning analysis at Epson, a Japanese multinational enterprise in Malaysia. His current research interests include China's industry development, especially strategic emerging industries, and China–ASEAN relations. He had published his works in *Review of Global Politics, Applied Econometrics and International Development, Journal of Overseas Chinese* and *Southeast Asian Studies*. He also frequently contributes commentaries to Singapore's largest Chinese daily *Lianhe Zaobao* and MediaCorp's FM95.8 Capital Radio.

LÜ Yue is an Assistant Professor of China Institute for WTO Studies, University of International Business and Economics. She received her

PhD in Economics from Nankai University. Her research fields cover global value chain, trade and finance. She has published a number of book chapters and over 20 articles in leading economics journals in both Chinese and English. Her articles have appeared in *International Interactions*, *Social Sciences in China* (Chinese and English editions), *World Economy* (in Chinese) and *Economics Research Journal* (in Chinese). She is a reviewer for *China and World Economy*. In addition, she was awarded a grant from the National Natural Science Foundation of China (2016–18) as principal investigator of her project.

WAN Jing is an Assistant Professor at the College of Management and Economics, Tianjin University. Prior that, she was a visiting research fellow at the EAI, National University of Singapore. She obtained her PhD in Economics from the National University of Singapore. She conducts research mainly in endogenous growth theory, macroeconomics and wealth inequality. Her publications have appeared in *Economic Letters*, *Economic Theory*, *China: An International Journal* and *Emerging Market Finance and Trade*.

CHEN Chien-Hsun is an Adviser with the Regional Development Study Center at Chung-Hua Institution for Economic Research, Taipei, Taiwan. He obtained his PhD in Economics from Oklahoma State University. He had taught at Wichita State University and formerly served as director of China Institute at Chung-Hua Institution for Economic Research. His research papers have appeared in journals such as *American Journal of Economics and Sociology*, *Asian Survey*, *China Economic Review*, *Economic Modelling*, *Eurasian Geography and Economics*, *Europe–Asia Studies*, *Journal of Comparative Economics*, *Journal of Contemporary Asia*, *Journal of Economic Policy Reform*, *Journal of Economic Studies*, *Journal of General Management*, *Journal of Macroeconomics*, *Pacific Accounting Review* and *Post-Communist Economies*.

CHIANG Min-Hua is Research Fellow at the EAI, National University of Singapore. She obtained her PhD in Economics from Université Pierre Mendès-France, now part of Université Grenoble Alpes. Prior to her current appointment in Singapore, she held research positions at National Chengchi University, Taiwan External Trade Development Council and Commerce Development Research Institute in Taipei. Her research interests include Asia-Pacific regionalism, trade and investment, and issues related to economic growth and development in East Asia. She is the author of *Post-Industrial Development in East Asia: Taiwan and South Korea in Comparison* (Palgrave Pivot, 2018), *Contemporary South Korean Economy: Challenges and Prospects* (World Scientific, 2017) and *China–Taiwan Rapprochement: the Political Economy of Cross-Strait Relations* (Routledge, 2016). Her articles have appeared in international peer-reviewed journals such as *The Pacific Review*, *Thunderbird International Business Review*, *China Perspectives*, *East Asian Policy: An International Quarterly*, *Journal of China Tourism Research*, *Revue de la Regulation* and *Journal of the Asia-Pacific Economy*.

ZHANG Yang is an Associate Professor of Business Economics at the Faculty of Business Administration, University of Macau. She obtained her PhD in Economics from Nanyang Technological University. Her research interests include economic dynamics, energy economics and Chinese economy. Her publications have appeared in leading international journals such as *Journal of Economic Dynamics and Control*, *Journal of Economic Behavior and Organization*, *Energy Economics*, *Applied Economics*, *Review of Development Economics* and *Economic Modelling*, among others. She was a visiting scholar of the University of Cambridge in 2013 and currently serves as the assistant editor of *Singapore Economic Review*.

CHOO Jaewoo is Professor of Chinese foreign policy in the Department of Chinese studies at Kyung Hee University, South Korea. He received his BA in Government from Wesleyan University, and his MA and PhD in International Relations from the School of International Studies at Peking University. Before teaching at Kyung Hee University, he worked as a researcher at a number of think tanks in Korea, such as National Security Policy Institute and Institute for International Trade at Korea International Trade Association. His research areas are Chinese foreign policy, multilateral security cooperation and China–North Korea relations. He is the author of *China's Foreign Policy: Concepts, Strategies and Diplomacy* (Elsevier, 2015) and *US–China Relations* (Lyeoksain, in Korean).

XING Yuqing is Professor of Economics at the National Graduate Institute for Policy Studies, Tokyo, Japan. He obtained his PhD in Economics from the University of Illinois at Urbana-Champaign. He provided consulting services to Asian Development Bank, the International Monetary Fund and Japan International Cooperation Agency. His research focuses on international trade, foreign direct investment, exchange rates and global value chains, for which he is a leading expert. His research on the iPhone and the China–US trade balance has been discussed widely in the global mainstream media, challenging conventional views on bilateral trade statistics and instigating a reform of trade statistics. He has also published widely in internationally refereed journals.

Introduction

Sarah Y TONG and KONG Tuan Yuen*

For more than half a century, East Asia has been the most dynamic and resilient economic region in the world. Following Japan's successful experience in its post-World War II reconstruction and industrialisation, a good number of East Asian economies flourished. The latest and perhaps the most extraordinary case is China's rapid economic development.

Since the late 1970s when the government initiated a policy of reform and opening up, China's economy has not only expanded rapidly to become the world's second largest, but also made remarkable transition. These include speedy industrialisation and significant expansion in urbanisation; a nearly complete shift from central planning to market driven business activities; and a transformation from a close economy to the world's largest trading nation.

Economic opening has been essential to China's outstanding performance of the past decades. As a result of the government's favourable policies, the amount of inward foreign direct investment surged, including those of export-orientation. These investments have played

---

* Sarah Y TONG is Senior Research Fellow at the East Asian Institute, National University of Singapore. KONG Tuan Yuen is Visiting Research Fellow at the same institute.

an important role in facilitating China's economic reform and growth; providing capital and technology, and access to world market; and inserting competitive pressure on domestic firms.

More significantly, China's has learnt and followed the successful experiences of other East Asian economies in their export-oriented development strategies. This has considerable implications for both China and its neighbours. On the one hand, China has benefitted tremendously through its participation in the growing linkages within East Asia, as well as between East Asia and the rest of the world. At the same time, engaging China has also promoted the region's economic cooperation and prosperity. In the meantime, China has become a key player and a central link in the formation and intensification of a regional production network and global supply chain.

However, this largely mutually beneficial economic relation between China and its East Asian neighbours is also facing challenges, especially since the late 2000s. First, since East Asia as a whole remained largely export-oriented and depends heavily on external demand from outside the region, further trade expansion is increasingly constrained. This inevitably leads to more competition among economies within and beyond East Asia. Second, since 2008, when the world economy was hard hit by a global financial crisis, growth in advanced economies has remained subdued. This has not only suppressed their overall demand but also spurred protectionist tendencies in these countries. As such, export from East Asia is threatened by weaker demand combined with stronger anti-globalisation forces. Third, as China aims to move its production activities upwards along the supply chain, it increases competition pressures upon those relatively more developed economies in the region, including Korea and Taiwan.

Nevertheless, the region seems committed to supporting economic opening, cooperation and integration. As the largest economy in the region, China pledged to play a leading role in promoting regional economic prosperity. First, China aims to enhance the growth of consumption and promote a more balanced trade. Meanwhile, the country is determined to further open its economy to trade and foreign investment, including those in services. Externally, China is also keen to assume a more active role in enhancing economic ties with its trading partners through its Belt and Road Initiative.

As a diverse and dynamic region, economic relations within East Asia have been resilient and served to facilitate economic development in the past decades. China's economic relations with its East Asian neighbours have been complex and nonetheless grown in strength. This edited volume will examine a number of China's key economic relations and the country's efforts in participating and promoting economic globalisation, as well as the overall development of East Asian economic integration.

Chapters 1 to 3 focus on China's importance and efforts in East Asian economic integration. In Chapter 1, the authors examine the changing patterns of growing East Asian production network. In particular, it looks at China's significant role in promoting further economic integration and development in East Asia, through outward investment, cooperation in infrastructure construction, trade and investment facilitation, and institution building in regional trade agreement.

In Chapter 2, the author reviews the process and achievement of China's efforts to internationalise its currency, the renminbi (RMB). Through concrete but cautious steps, including the launch of the Shanghai-Hong Kong stock market connect in 2014, interest rate liberalisation in 2015 and the establishment of RMB offshore markets, China has made significant progress in RMB internationalisation. This is reflected in part by the inclusion of RMB by the International Monetary Fund in its Special Drawing Right in 2016.

Chapter 3 evaluates the efforts to internationalise Chinese firms, including the Go Global initiative of the government since the early 2000s. As the amount of China's outward direct investment increases, the composition of the investment has also evolved. Initially led by government-backed state-owned enterprises, more outward investment is now conducted by the non-state sector. Increasingly, the aim is to acquire technology and advanced Research and Development (R&D) capabilities.

Chapters 4 to 8 review China's economic relations with Taiwan (Chapter 4), Hong Kong (Chapter 5), ASEAN (Chapter 6), Korea (Chapter 7) and Japan (Chapter 8). In Chapter 4, the author recapitulates the several phases in the development of cross-strait economic relations, which started in the 1980s. While bilateral economic ties in both trade and investment are strong, the author highlighted various challenges. In particular, the Tsai Ing-wen government is wary of the growing presence of mainland investment and prospect of higher economic dependence on the economy of the Mainland. Greater efforts have been made to enhance Taiwan's economic relations with other economies especially those in Southeast Asia.

In assessing economic relations between Chinese mainland and Hong Kong, Chapter 5 focuses on the role of CEPA (Closer Economic Partnership Arrangement), between the two. Signed in 2003, CEPA was essential to sustaining Hong Kong's economy and to enhance bilateral economic relations after the outbreak of SARS (Severe Acute Respiratory Syndrome). By reducing tariffs and providing easier access to the mainland markets, CEPA gives Hong Kong businesses a competitive edge over businesses from elsewhere. More importantly, the two sides have enhanced their financial integration through initiatives such as the Shanghai-Hong Kong Stock Connect, generating additional benefits for both sides.

Chapter 6 considers China's economic relations with ASEAN, the economic grouping of 10 Southeast Asian countries. The authors highlight the growing bilateral ties, including those in trade and two-way investment. They further call attention to the recent trend in bilateral economic relations. These include rising trade imbalances and the more rapid growth in China's trade with ASEAN's newer members, namely, Cambodia, Laos, Myanmar and Vietnam. The authors also stress the significance of continued efforts to strengthen economic cooperation and regional economic integration through various institutions and initiatives such as the Belt and Road Initiative, Asian Infrastructural Investment Bank and the Silk Road Fund.

Chapter 7 looks at the economic relations between China and South Korea. The author cautions that while trade and investment relations between the two are strong, future economic relations may be sabotaged by tensions in other areas. In particular, conflicts of interest and ensuing diplomatic tensions may hinder efforts towards economic integration. Despite growing intra-regional trade, deepening division of labour, expanding production network and the security predicament have become serious obstacles and delayed China-Korea economic integration. Most significantly, heightened political and diplomatic tension between the two after Korea decided to deploy THAAD (Terminal High Altitude Area Defence) system could have serious and lasting impact on economic integration in East Asia.

Chapter 8 concentrates on the development of Sino-Japanese economic relations. The author highlights that the two sides have established very strong bilateral economic ties in the absence of any formal institutional setting. The author further identifies a key feature of bilateral trade, where a large portion of China's exports to Japan are process exports in nature. The author discerns several recent trends in bilateral economic relations. For example, Japan's direct investment in China is shifting from export-oriented towards domestic market-oriented. Chinese businesses have also increased their mergers and acquisitions (M&A) in Japan in search of strategic asset and intellectual property. Chinese tourists to Japan have also risen significantly.

Chapters 9 discusses the political economy aspect of East Asian economic integration. The authors describe the origins and processes of East Asian economic integration from the Flying Geese model to the numerous free trade arrangements involving the region. The authors believe that economic cooperation and integration has served the region well by transforming it into the most dynamic and rapidly growth region. The region has also been among the most active in promoting multilateral institutions to enhance economic integration, in addition to safeguarding peace and stability. Most significantly, ASEAN has played a central role in facilitating regional initiatives such as Regional Comprehensive Economic Partnership and the Free Trade Area of the Asia Pacific.

Chapter 1

China and East Asia Production Network

LÜ Yue and Sarah Y TONG*

In recent decades, as economic globalisation deepens, the patterns of production organisation have evolved considerably and, in particular, regional production networks have greatly intensified. It is generally thought that there are currently three regional production networks, namely "Factory North America" consisting of the United States and Mexico, "Factory Europe" comprising Germany and Eastern European countries, as well as "Factory Asia" making up of China and other East Asian economies.[1] There is no doubt that "Factory Asia" has become a key third pole of the world economy. While globalisation has greatly contributed to the deepening of East Asian economic integration, East Asia's industrial structure has undergone significant changes and new value chains are taking shape.

East Asian production network originated from the so-called "flying geese model".[2] Led by Japan, the first industrialised nation in Asia,

---

* LÜ Yue is Associate Professor of China Institute for WTO Studies, University of International Business and Economics. She was a Visiting Scholar at the East Asian Institute, National University of Singapore. Sarah Y Tong is Senior Research Fellow at the East Asian Institute, National University of Singapore.
[1] Richard Baldwin and Javier Lopez-Gonzalez, "Supply-Chain Trade: A Portrait of Global Patterns and Several Testable Hypotheses", *NBER Working Paper* No. w18957, 2013.
[2] Liu Zhongwei. "East Asian Production Network, the New Trend of Global Value Chain Integration and Cooperation in East Asia Region" (Dongya shengchan wangluo, quanqiu

economic development trickled down to other East Asian countries as they were gradually incorporated into Japan-led regional manufacturing and trade activities. Up to the 1980s, production was centred largely around Japanese firms, located both in Japan and in other parts of East Asia. Production and trading networks, in particular, had forged integration of regional economies such as Hong Kong, South Korea, Singapore and Taiwan. After the Chinese government's launch of economic reform and opening up in the late 1970s, the country became a major destination for foreign investment. In the ensuing decades, Asia's production and trade networks further expanded and consolidated. Since the mid-2000s, China gradually surpassed the original core countries, such as Japan, becoming a key link of the East Asian production network.[3] Overtime, East Asian economies gradually developed production modes with distinct characteristics, including fragmented production and vertical specialisation within a new China-centric production network.

China's Changing Role in the East Asian Production Network

After over three decades of rapid growth, China has developed into the world's second-largest economy, and a key engine of growth for Asia and the world economy. In 1980, China's nominal gross domestic product (GDP) was only US$0.19 trillion, or less than 20% of Japan's GDP. In 2010, China surpassed Japan becoming Asia's largest and the world's second-largest economy, behind the United States. In 2015, China's GDP amounted to US$11.01 trillion, eight times larger than its GDP in 2000 in nominal term and more than three-fifths of US' GDP.[4] As its economy expands, China's role in East Asia becomes increasingly

---

jiazhilian zhenghe yu Dongya quyu hezuo de xinzouxiang), *Contemporary Asia-Pacific*, no. 4, 2014.

[3] Dieter Ernst and Paolo Guerrieri, "International Production Networks and Changing Trade Patterns in East Asia: The Case of the Electronics Industry", *Oxford Development Studies*, vol. 26, 1998, pp. 191–212.

[4] The World Bank, at <http://data.worldbank.org> (accessed 14 February 2017).

Table 1. Per Capita GDP and its Growth in East and Southeast Asia

	GDP per Capita (US$)		Growth of GDP per Capita (%)	
	2000–2007	2008–2015	2000–2007	2008–2015
Japan	34,678.70	40,171.71	−0.01	−2.36
Singapore	27,022.25	49,488.72	0.07	3.78
Hong Kong SAR	26,019.41	36,044.30	0.03	4.13
Brunei	25,330.19	40,333.46	0.09	−1.79
Macao SAR	22,209.35	67,998.15	0.14	9.82
South Korea	16,318.73	23,972.57	0.10	3.88
Taiwan	15,451.00	20,334.48	0.02	2.59
Malaysia	5,154.50	9,560.08	0.08	1.90
Thailand	2,647.54	5,393.58	0.10	3.97
China	1,558.49	5,775.15	0.16	13.03
Indonesia	1,245.07	3,214.21	0.13	5.72
Philippines	1,170.06	2,438.68	0.07	6.31
Viet Nam	582.35	1,610.60	0.13	8.94
North Korea	509.17	—	0.04	—
Laos	438.95	1,351.20	0.12	11.23
Cambodia	420.97	920.59	0.11	6.56
Myanmar	225.76	976.54	0.13	12.76

Source: The United Nations Conference on Trade and Development (UNCTAD).

significant. In 2015, China's GDP accounted for nearly 56% of East and Southeast Asia's combined GDP, up from less than 20% in 2000.[5]

In terms of per capita GDP, China ranked No. 10 among the 17 economies in East and Southeast Asia between 2008 and 2015, after Japan, Singapore, Hong Kong, Brunei, Macao, South Korea, Taiwan, Malaysia and Thailand (Table 1).[6] Nonetheless, China's per capita GDP growth had outpaced most other economies in the region. In

---

[5] The United Nations Conference on Trade and Development, at <http://unctadstat.unctad.org/wds/TableViewer/tableView.aspx> (accessed 14 February 2017).
[6] In this chapter's context, East and Southeast Asia consist of 17 economies — China, Hong Kong Special Administrative Region (SAR), Japan, Macao SAR, North Korea,

addition, the CLMV (Cambodia, Laos, Myanmar and Vietnam) countries have performed relatively stronger since the late 2000s and are catching up to reach middle-income level, albeit from a low base. China has meanwhile joined the upper-middle-income group.

China at the centre of an expanding intra-East Asian trade

There are two important features of China's trade with other East Asian economies. First, rapid growth in trade of components and intermediate goods. Second, large and rising trade deficits between China and East Asian countries, while China's trade surplus with other countries had also expanded.

Despite being known as the "world factory", China actually imports large volume of intermediate goods and ships out final products in the form of processing exports. In recent years, trade in intermediate goods accounted for about 80% of total imports (Figure 1). In addition, East and Southeast Asia are China's important suppliers of components and intermediate goods, providing over 40% of China's imports on average between 2000 and 2013. However, this figure had decreased over the years to below 40% in 2014 (Figure 2).

It is noteworthy that East and Southeast Asia's bilateral trade volume with China remains large although their share in China's imports of intermediate goods has declined to some extent. As is shown in Figure 3, China's exports to countries in East Asia, excluding Hong Kong, rose from US$54 billion in 2000 to US$257 billion in 2014, an increase of 3.7 times. Meanwhile, China's imports from the region recorded an even faster growth from US$65 billion to US$356 billion, a fivefold increase. China consequently incurred a sizeable trade deficit, especially since 2010, often amounting to over US$100 billion in recent years.

Meanwhile, China's trade with countries in Southeast Asia has expanded at an even faster rate since the early 2000s, although from

---

South Korea and Taiwan in East Asia; and Brunei, Cambodia, Indonesia, Laos, Malaysia, Myanmar, the Philippines, Singapore, Thailand and Vietnam in Southeast Asia.

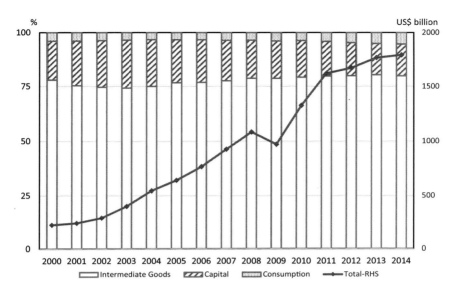

Figure 1. Chinese Commodity Imports: Total and Share by Commodity Groups
Source: UNCTAD Statistical Database and Broad Economic Categories Classification.

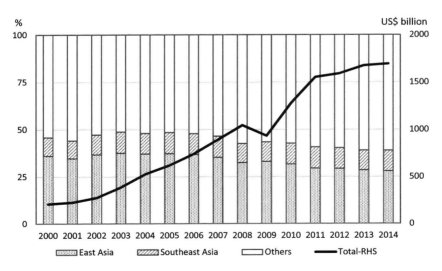

Figure 2. Chinese Imports of Intermediate Goods Total and Share by Regions
Source: UNCTAD Statistical Database and Broad Economic Categories Classification.

Panel A: China's Trade with East Asia (Excluding HKSAR)

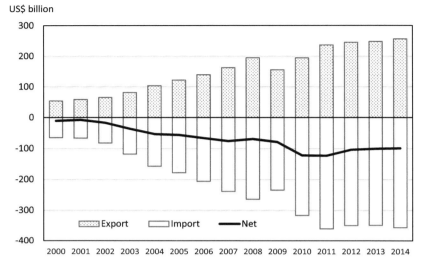

Panel B: China's Trade with Southeast Asia

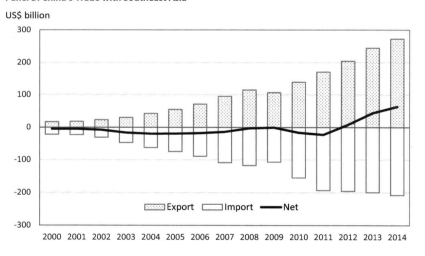

Figure 3. China's Trade in Goods with Regional Partners, 2000–2014

Note: The data excludes China's trade with Hong Kong.

Source: Calculated by authors based on data from World Integrated Trade Solution (WITS) database.

a smaller base. Between 2000 and 2014, China's exports to the region rose from US$17 billion to US$272 billion (an increase of more than 15-fold) and its imports from the region from US$22 billion to US$208 billion (an increase of more than nine-fold). As a result of faster export growth that outpaced import growth, China had turned its trade balance with Southeast Asia from deficit to surplus in 2012, which has since further increased to hit US$64 billion in 2014.

If trade with Hong Kong is included, China continues to sustain trade surplus with East Asian countries as a group. This is due largely to Hong Kong's strategic importance as a gateway for China's commodity export, and also as logistics and warehousing services suppliers to China. Many multinational corporations set up regional headquarters in Hong Kong, serving the Asia-Pacific regional trade and providing commercial services.[7]

China, a key foreign direct investment (FDI) recipient in East Asia

Following Deng Xiaoping's southern tour in early 1992, which reinvigorated China's economic reform, the country soon became a key recipient of cross-border direct investment. As is shown in Figure 4, foreign direct investment (FDI) inflows rose rapidly from US$11 billion in 1992 to a pre-crisis peak of US$108 billion in 2008, an average annual growth of over 15%. After a significant drop to below US$100 billion in 2009, FDI to China grew again at a slower pace to reach US$129 billion in 2014 and US$135 billion in 2015. Overall, China has been a top FDI recipient and was ranked the world's third-largest in 2015, behind the United States and Hong Kong. By 2015, China's FDI stock amounted to over US$1.2 trillion, accounting for nearly 5% of the world's total, and ranking it in the fourth place.

---

[7] Pascal Lamy and Takashi Shiraishi, *Trade Patterns and Global Value Chains in East Asia: From Trade in Goods to Trade in Tasks*, Geneva: IDE-JETRO and WTO, 2011.

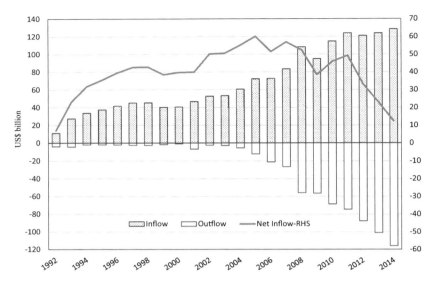

Figure 4. China's Inward and Outward Foreign Direct Investment (US$ billion)
Source: Calculated by authors based on data from UNCTAD.

Meanwhile, China was not a major player in outbound FDI until the early 2000s. Outward FDI (OFDI) began to expand since 2003, when the government launched the so-called "going out" strategy and encouraged large state-owned enterprises (SOEs) to invest abroad. China's annual OFDI surged from less than US$3 billion in 2003 to US$127 billion in 2015, an annual increase of more than 40%. While China remains a net recipient of direct investment, the gap has shrunk rapidly to around US$7.4 billion in 2015.

More importantly, East and Southeast Asia are key to China's two-way investment flows. China's main sources of inward FDI are East and Southeast Asia, making up to more than 80% of the total in recent years (Figure 5). In 2014, for example, FDI from East and Southeast Asian economies were US$92.1 billion and US$6.3 billion, respectively.

Specifically, Hong Kong has been China's largest source of FDI. In 2014, investment from Hong Kong amounted to US$81.3 billion

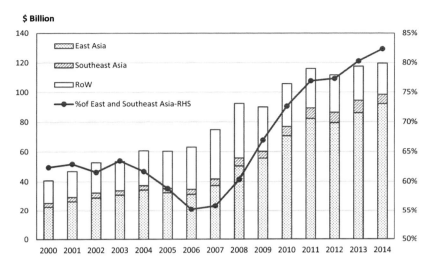

Figure 5. Annual FDI to China: By Main Regions and Share of East and Southeast Asia

Notes: Region refers to East Asia and Southeast Asia. RoW denotes the rest of the world.
Source: Bilateral FDI Statistics based on UNCTAD database; National Bureau of Statistics of China database.

Table 2. China's Top Asian Sources of FDI

	Year	Rank	US$ Billion	Year	Rank	US$ Billion
Hong Kong	2014	1	81.27	2005	1	35.72
Singapore	2014	2	5.83	2005	4	2.20
Japan	2014	3	4.32	2005	2	6.53
South Korea	2014	4	3.97	2005	3	5.17
Taiwan	2014	5	2.02	2005	5	2.15

Source: International Trade Centre (ITC) Investment Map, National Bureau of Statistics of China database.

(Table 2), or more than two-thirds of the total. Meanwhile, Singapore has in recent years overtaken South Korea and Japan to become China's second-largest source of FDI inflows among Asian investors, investing nearly US$6 billion in 2014.

China — the Key to Economic Development and Integration in East Asia

China's rapid economic growth has significant positive effect on East Asian economies and is imperative to the rapid intensification of the East Asian production network.[8] China's combined trade in intermediate goods with East Asia and Southeast Asia rose from US$158.68 billion in 2002 to US$837.14 billion in 2014, an increase of 4.3 times (Table 3). However, East Asia and Southeast Asia's share in China's total

Table 3. Total Amount and Share of China's Intermediates Trade with Regional Partners (US$ billion and %)

	With East Asia		With Southeast Asia		With Others		(1) + (3)
	(1)	(2)	(3)	(4)	(5)	(6)	(1) + (3) + (5)
2002	120.27	–12.30	38.80	–11.62	135.94	–27.35	54%
2003	157.60	–19.48	53.66	–19.45	191.56	–41.59	52%
2004	208.05	–24.86	73.18	–22.67	277.84	–60.06	50%
2005	250.02	–22.73	89.82	–25.02	350.08	–60.11	49%
2006	294.68	–17.21	109.98	–27.56	449.50	–48.55	47%
2007	347.00	–13.86	137.60	–31.67	588.02	–54.13	45%
2008	383.92	–1.40	148.75	–23.44	776.61	–95.09	41%
2009	320.66	–31.39	128.89	–27.54	633.39	–127.59	42%
2010	414.32	–42.08	185.80	–49.87	896.05	–183.05	40%
2011	478.50	–31.75	235.59	–64.62	1145.82	–260.11	38%
2012	501.53	–7.93	250.86	–47.19	1173.67	–286.35	39%
2013	549.62	30.28	278.32	–31.45	1238.33	–304.86	40%
2014	532.50	–2.51	308.25	–20.80	1299.50	–254.61	39%

Notes: Columns (1), (3) and (5) denote total trade in intermediate goods (imports plus exports); columns (2), (4) and (6) denote net exports for intermediate goods (exports minus imports).

Source: United Nations Comtrade database.

---

[8] Liu Zhongwei, "East Asian Production Network, the New Trend of Global Value Chain Integration and Cooperation in East Asia Region".

trade in intermediate goods during the same period dropped from 54% to 39%. Nevertheless, China has continued to be a net importer of intermediate goods, importing growing volume of intermediate goods from other sources.[9] It is therefore evident that China, through greater trade and closer regional production network, has helped to propel the growth in its neighbouring economies.

China's trade dependence on East and Southeast Asia has meanwhile declined, as the country diversifies its trade and upgrades its industries. The share of China's imports from East and Southeast Asia including Hong Kong declined from 44.2% in 2000 to 31.8% in 2014 (Table 4).

Table 4. Import–Export Matrix: China/Hong Kong/East Asia and Southeast Asia (US$ Billion, %)

	Exporter				
	2000				
		China	Hong Kong	East Asia	Southeast Asia	ROW
Importer	China	—	9.4 (4.3%)	64.8 (29.7%)	22.2 (10.2%)	121.5
	Hong Kong	91.7 (24.0%)	—	36.4	22.3	63.5
	East Asia	68.4 (17.9%)	3.1	—	76.4	389.0
	Southeast Asia	18.0 (4.7%)	9.1	87.2	—	244.7
	ROW	204.7	—	—	—	—
	2014				
	China	—	12.8 (0.7%)	356.0 (19.6%)	208.2 (11.5%)	1,236.4
	Hong Kong	268.2 (13.6%)	—	62.8	76.5	192.8
	East Asia	273.5 (13.9%)	3.7	—	166.8	894.1
	Southeast Asia	209.9 (10.6%)	13.9	186.7	—	798.5
	ROW	1,222.1	—	—	—	—

Notes: In this table, East Asia does not include Hong Kong; the data reporter is China.

Source: Calculated by authors based on data from World Integrated Trade Solution (WITS) database.

---

[9] Tang Haiyan and Zhang Kuaiqing, "Rise of China and the East Asian Production Network Reconfiguration" (Zhongguo jueqi yu Dongya shengchan wangluo chongggou), *China Industrial Economy*, vol. 12, 2008.

Similarly, the region's share in China's exports also fell, from 46.5% to 38.1%. Conversely, China's importance to its neighbours as a market for exports and a source of imports rose significantly. In 2000, East Asian economies' share of exports to China accounted for 6.6% of the total but this went up to 27.7% in 2014. Similarly, East Asian economies' imports from China rose from 16.0% in 2000 to 23.8% in 2014.

East Asia, the primary destination of China's outward direct investment

As a developing nation, China's outward direct investment (OFDI) became sizeable only since the early 2000s and has grown to substantial levels since 2008 (Figure 6). China's official data has shown that East and Southeast Asia were the primary destinations for China's OFDI, accounting for 68% of the total in 2012. However, over US$50 billion, or 86% of Chinese OFDI to East and Southeast Asia valued at US$60 billion, landed in Hong Kong. There is a possibility

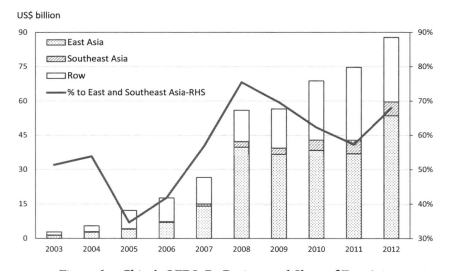

Figure 6.   China's OFDI: By Regions and Share of East Asia

Notes: % of the World to Region, where "region" includes East Asia and Southeast Asia. ROW denotes rest of the world.

Source: Bilateral FDI Statistics based on UNCTAD database.

Table 5. The OFDI's Destination of Five Largest Asian Investors (2014)

Asian Investors	Top Three Destinations	US$ Billion	Share of Economy's Outflows (%)
Japan	Australia	9.46	17.7
	Indonesia	9.39	17.6
	China	8.46	15.8
Singapore	Indonesia	12.25	32.9
	China	7.25	19.5
	Hong Kong	3.24	8.7
China (including Hong Kong)	Singapore	3.85	25.3
	Australia	3.01	19.8
	Japan	1.13	7.5
South Korea	China	3.49	53.0
	Indonesia	0.82	12.4
	Viet Nam	0.72	11.0
Malaysia	Singapore	2.49	45.8
	Indonesia	0.90	16.5
	Australia	0.75	13.7

Source: ADB, *Asian Economic Integration Research Report 2015*.

that a large portion of China's OFDI to Hong Kong was channelled to another location, and the cited OFDI values to Hong Kong could be an overestimate.

According to a report by Asian Development Bank (ADB),[10] China (including Hong Kong) is Asia's third-largest source of OFDI (Table 5). An interesting characteristic of OFDI from Asia is that it is largely concentrated within the region and Australia. China has invested mainly in the more developed Asian countries such as Singapore and Japan. It is also a top host to its neighbours' FDI, South Korea being the largest investor, followed by Singapore, the second-largest and Japan, the third-largest in 2014.

---

[10] Asian Development Bank, "How Can Special Economic Zones Catalyze Economic Development?", *Asian Economic Integration Report* 2015.

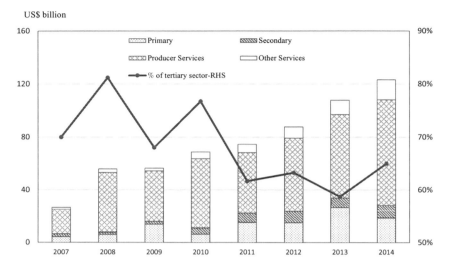

Figure 7. Chinese OFDI by Sectors and Production of Producer Services
Sources: Information and Communication Technology (ICT) Investment Map; and National Bureau of Statistics of China database.

Chinese outward investment is mainly in tertiary industries, especially producer services (Figure 7). China's OFDI in services rose from US$20 billion in 2007 to US$95 billion in 2014, accounting for over three-fifth of the total. OFDI in the primary sector, particularly the resource-related industries, grew from US$4.3 billion in 2007 to US$26.6 billion, the peak value, in 2013. Between 2007 and 2014, primary investment totalled US$105.7 billion, or around 17.6% of China's overall OFDI. China's OFDI in manufacturing is relatively small and insignificant, constituting less than 10% of the total.

Forming a China-centric Asian production network

Cross-border production collaboration and trade in parts and intermediate goods have brought sustained growth in East and Southeast Asia, resulting in the formation of industrial clusters and a dynamic and diverse supply chain.[11] "Factory Asia" is thus a unique mode of production that features an extensive and evolving "network".[12]

More significantly, the network's centre of gravity has clearly shifted in recent years. In 2000, Japan was the lead supplier to regional economies of intermediate goods, with extensive linkages with China, South Korea, Taiwan, Malaysia, the Philippines and Thailand in both inputs and outputs (Table 6). In 2011, Japan's lead position was largely taken over by China, which has evidently become the key link in the tightly connected East Asian production network.

Japan, Malaysia and Singapore had been the core members of the East Asian production network since the 1980s, until China gradually gained significance to overtake the core members in the early 2000s. In 2000, mainland China's share of intermediate goods in Hong Kong's, Japan's and South Korea's total input of intermediate goods was 41%, 25% and 16%, respectively. In 2011, these figures went up to 54%, 44% and 39%, respectively. In addition, China is an important supplier for intermediate goods to other Southeast Asian countries such as Vietnam and Cambodia. Imports from China accounted for 11% and 12% of Vietnam's and Cambodia's total imports of intermediate goods in 2000, respectively, and these subsequently increased to 32% and 37% in 2011, making China the most important suppliers of intermediate goods.

Significant impact on East Asia's employment

Deepening economic interdependence and associated growth can have substantial impact on employment in the region. Employment is in turn affected by the regions' overall development and degree of connectedness. Growing East Asian integration enhances trade among regional economies as well as between the region and the rest of the

---

[11] David Roland-Holst, Azis Iwan and Liu Li-Gang, "Regionalism and Globalism: East and Southeast Asian Trade Relations in Wake of China's WTO Accession", ADB Institute Research Paper Series, no. XX, 2003.
[12] Richard Baldwin and Javier Lopez-Gonzalez, "Supply-Chain Trade: A Portrait of Global Patterns and Several Testable Hypotheses", *NBER Working Paper* no. w18957, 2013.

Table 6. Flows of Intermediate Inputs and Share in Total among East Asian Economies, 2000 and 2011

2000

	CHN	HKG	JPN	KOR	TWN	BRN	IDN	KHM	MYS	PHL	SGP	THA	VNM
CHN	0%	41%	25%	16%	8%	6%	10%	12%	6%	5%	8%	8%	11%
HKG	7%	0%	2%	2%	4%	2%	2%	11%	3%	5%	4%	3%	2%
JPN	35%	19%	0%	46%	50%	12%	28%	3%	36%	31%	29%	42%	19%
KOR	20%	12%	17%	0%	13%	6%	13%	8%	9%	16%	7%	7%	17%
TWN	19%	12%	13%	8%	0%	12%	6%	25%	10%	13%	7%	8%	15%
BRN	0%	0%	2%	1%	0%	0%	0%	0%	0%	0%	0%	2%	0%
IDN	3%	1%	13%	9%	4%	2%	0%	4%	4%	5%	10%	4%	3%
KHM	0%	0%	0%	0%	0%	0%	0%	0%	0%	0%	0%	0%	0%
MYS	5%	3%	12%	8%	8%	26%	9%	7%	0%	8%	24%	11%	4%
PHL	1%	1%	3%	2%	3%	0%	1%	0%	3%	0%	2%	2%	1%
SGP	4%	8%	5%	6%	6%	31%	24%	6%	22%	11%	0%	11%	21%
THA	3%	3%	6%	2%	3%	3%	6%	20%	6%	5%	6%	0%	7%
VNM	1%	0%	1%	1%	1%	1%	2%	4%	1%	1%	1%	2%	0%

2011

	CHN	HKG	JPN	KOR	TWN	BRN	IDN	KHM	MYS	PHL	SGP	THA	VNM
CHN	0%	54%	44%	39%	29%	15%	23%	37%	23%	23%	22%	24%	32%
HKG	4%	0%	1%	2%	2%	2%	1%	3%	2%	1%	5%	2%	1%
JPN	28%	12%	0%	30%	35%	11%	13%	2%	18%	15%	19%	30%	12%
KOR	25%	7%	13%	0%	12%	4%	18%	7%	7%	14%	11%	9%	17%
TWN	17%	8%	6%	6%	0%	3%	5%	13%	8%	12%	10%	6%	11%
BRN	0%	0%	2%	1%	0%	0%	1%	0%	0%	0%	0%	0%	1%
IDN	4%	3%	12%	8%	6%	6%	0%	2%	11%	9%	10%	7%	3%
KHM	0%	0%	0%	0%	0%	0%	0%	0%	0%	0%	0%	0%	0%
MYS	8%	1%	8%	4%	5%	24%	11%	4%	0%	7%	12%	10%	6%
PHL	2%	1%	2%	2%	2%	1%	1%	0%	2%	0%	3%	3%	1%
SGP	4%	11%	4%	4%	5%	31%	15%	3%	17%	9%	0%	7%	5%
THA	5%	3%	6%	3%	3%	4%	9%	11%	10%	8%	6%	0%	9%
VNM	2%	0%	3%	2%	1%	0%	2%	17%	3%	2%	1%	2%	0%

Notes: The percentage values in the table are shares of column economies' intermediate inputs from row economies in column economies' inputs of intermediate goods.

CHN: Chinese Mainland; HKG: Hong Kong; JPN: Japan; KOR: South Korea; TWN: Taiwan; BRN: Brunei; IDN: Indonesia; KHM: Cambodia; MYS: Malaysia; PHL: the Philippines; SGP: Singapore; THA: Thailand; and VNM: Vietnam.

Source: Calculated by authors using data from World Input Output Database (WIOD).

world. China's involvement as a large economy brought additional benefits to its neighbours in terms of access to its huge domestic market, push for economic transformation and increased employment opportunities. Indeed, China's economic opening had presumably contributed considerably to East Asia's job creation. In 2000, for economies like Indonesia, Japan, South Korea, Malaysia, Taiwan, the Philippines, Singapore and Thailand, the creation of 3.3 million jobs can be credited to their economic ties with China (Table 7). In 2005,

Table 7. Jobs Related to Cross-Border Trade, as of 2000 and 2005 (in thousands)

2000	CHN	IDN	JPN	KOR	MYS	TWN	PHL	SGP	THA	Total
CHN	—	911	18,817	3,406	916	1,425	362	839	992	27,668
IDN	1,138	—	3,733	702	612	591	244	525	399	7,944
JPN	420	66	—	264	112	285	63	94	123	1,427
KOR	340	32	373	—	30	88	31	25	29	948
MYS	201	47	569	109	—	111	50	260	84	1,431
TWN	373	22	318	59	42	—	25	21	38	898
PHL	314	30	1,506	228	127	213	—	52	98	2,568
SGP	33	8	43	18	31	20	14	—	16	183
THA	473	149	1,539	182	278	243	123	247	—	3,234
Total	3,292	1,265	26,898	4,968	2,148	2,976	912	2,063	1,779	46,301

2005	CHN	IDN	JPN	KOR	MYS	TWN	PHL	SGP	THA	Total
CHN	—	1,943	23,266	5,521	1,055	2,617	481	844	2,032	37,759
IDN	1,795	—	3,032	746	610	417	166	686	508	7,960
JPN	1,003	110	—	425	62	349	57	46	204	2,256
KOR	727	44	330	—	20	71	18	12	45	1,267
MYS	1,030	170	776	221	—	156	62	185	300	2,900
TWN	818	31	308	83	32	—	33	13	55	1,373
PHL	1,565	107	1,249	282	101	204	—	34	238	3,780
SGP	82	59	69	58	27	15	12	—	23	345
THA	1,203	422	1,568	246	249	213	94	122	—	4,117
Total	8,223	2,886	30,598	7,582	2,156	4,042	923	1,942	3,405	61,757

Source: Institute of Developing Economies, *The Asian International Input–Output Tables*, 2000 and 2005.

Table 8. Intra-Regional Job Creation from Trade by Sectors (in Thousands and %)

	Primary	Secondary	Service	% Primary	% Secondary	% Service
CHN	32,624	25,952	30,725	36.5%	29.1%	34.4%
IDN	5,751	1,967	4,664	46.4%	15.9%	37.7%
THA	3,614	1,507	1,414	55.3%	23.1%	21.6%
PHL	2,021	1,161	2,204	37.5%	21.6%	40.9%
MSY	953	1,640	2,351	19.3%	33.2%	47.6%
JPN	454	1,722	1,833	11.3%	43.0%	45.7%
TWN	128	1,173	664	6.5%	59.7%	33.8%
KOR	259	793	813	13.9%	42.5%	43.6%
SGP	7	267	180	1.5%	58.8%	39.6%

Source: Institute of Developing Economies, *The Asian International Input–Output Tables*, 2005.

job opportunities increased in these economies with 8.2 million jobs created. Conversely, in 2005, 37.8 million jobs were created in China — a substantial increase from 28.7 million jobs created in 2000 — and this can be attributed to its economic linkages with these economies.

Intraregional trade also facilitates job creation. China's trade with countries in the East and Southeast Asia had helped generate nearly 90 million jobs as of 2005, over one-third of which were in the primary sector and another one-third in services (Table 8). The sectoral allocation of trade-generated jobs varied across countries. For example, in Indonesia and Thailand, the primary sector had the largest share of job created, while in the Philippines, Malaysia, Japan and South Korea, majority of the jobs were created in the services sector. In Taiwan and Singapore, the secondary sector had the largest share of trade-related job creation.

Enhanced connectivity through infrastructure construction

Good infrastructure is essential in promoting East Asia's economic interconnectivity. Infrastructure in East Asia has greatly improved in

26 | CHINA AND EAST ASIAN ECONOMIC INTEGRATION

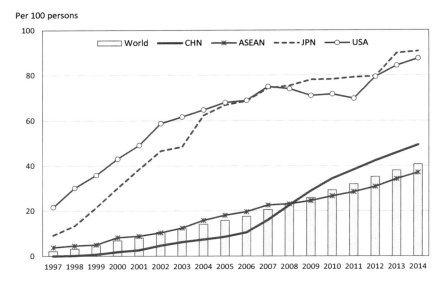

Figure 8. Internet Usage of Selected Economies

Source: The World Bank database.

recent decades. The number of internet users in the region had risen significantly from 0.03 per hundred people in 1997 to 49.3 per hundred in 2014 (Figure 8). The penetration rate, while higher than the world's average at 41 per hundred, is still considered low compared to that of developed countries such as the United States (87.4) and Japan (90.6).

For many East Asian countries, the number of registered air cargo containers also underwent substantial increase in recent years (Table 9). China reported significant increase, from 570,000 in 2000 to 3.4 million in 2014, far outpacing other countries in the region.

Huge potentials remain for infrastructure investment in East and Southeast Asia. Studies have shown that a good and comprehensive infrastructure is often associated with better economic performances.[13] The ADB reported that Asian economies need huge investment in

---

[13] See, for example, David A. Aschauer, "Is Public Expenditure Productive?", *Journal of Monetary Economics*, vol. 23, no. 2, 1989, pp. 177–200; Ernst R. Berndt and Bengt Hansson, "Measuring the Contribution of Public Infrastructure Capital in Sweden", *National Bureau of Economic Research* no. W3842, 1991; Catherine J. Morrison and

Table 9. Number of Registered Air Transport Containers in Selected East Asian Countries, 2000 and 2014 (in million)

	2014	2000	Increase (2000 to 2014)
CHN	3.36	0.57	2.78
JPN	0.93	0.65	0.28
IDN	0.70	0.16	0.54
MYS	0.44	0.17	0.27
KOR	0.38	0.23	0.15
THA	0.32	0.10	0.22
PHL	0.23	0.04	0.18
SGP	0.19	0.07	0.12
VNM	0.14	0.03	0.12
MMR	0.03	0.01	0.02
LAO	0.01	0.01	0.01
BRN	0.01	0.01	0.00
KHM	0.01	0.00	0.01

Source: The World Bank Database.

infrastructure amounting to US$8 trillion domestically and US$300 billion in regional infrastructure between 2010 and 2020 in order to reach the world average in infrastructure development. There is a big financing gap to achieve this goal.[14] In fact, efforts have been made by China to help bridge the gap, as is evident in its commitment to promote East Asian regional cooperation through initiatives such as the Belt and Road Initiatives (BRI) and the Asian Infrastructure Investment Bank (AIIB). By working with other international and regional financial institutions such as the World Bank and ADB, AIIB could support the region's infrastructure development by providing infrastructure financing, thus enhancing economic integration in the region.

Amy E. Schwartz, "State Infrastructure and Productive Performance", *National Bureau of Economic Research* no. W3981, 1992.

[14] See <http://www.adb.org/zh/news/adb-signs-first-ever-ppp-co-advisory-agreement-global-banks> (accessed 4 May 2015).

Trade agreements in East Asia

The East and Southeast Asian region has in recent years become a new growth pole for the global economy. Free trade agreements (FTAs) were therefore actively promoted and signed. Intricate protocols and overlapping memberships have thus led to the so-called "Asian noodle bowl" phenomenon.[15] More recently, there were indications of competition and rivalry between the Trans-Pacific Partnership (TPP) agreement and the Regional Comprehensive Economic Partnership (RCEP). Although the recent US withdrawal added uncertainties to the future of TPP, continued efforts were made by the remaining parties to salvage the agreement. As clearly shown in Table 10, many economies in the region are involved in multiple bilateral FTAs, as well as in negotiations of regional trade pack. For example, China has bilateral FTAs with Singapore, Thailand, and South Korea, as well as an ASEAN Plus One

Table 10. Free Trade Agreement Matrix of East Asia

	BRN	IDN	MYS	PHL	SGP	THA	VNM	CHN	KOR	JPN
CHN					•	•			•	
KOR		○			•		○	•		
JPN	•	•	•	•	•	•	•		○	
TPP	√		√		√		√			√
RCEP	√	√	√	√	√	√	√	√	√	√

Notes: • indicates that two countries have signed and implemented bilateral free trade agreements;
○ indicates that bilateral free trade agreement is under negotiation;
√ denotes the country has joined the TPP negotiations and RCEP member;
shading in light grey indicates that the country has signed the "10+1" (or ASEAN Plus One) trade agreement;
dashed boxes denotes FTAs still under negotiation.

Source: Guo Ting and Sheng Bin. "The Asia-Pacific Regional Economic Integration, Transnational Production Game and China's Strategic Choice" (Yatai quyu jingji yitihua boyi yu Zhongguo de zhanlue xuanze), *World Economics and Politics*, no. 10, 2014.

---

[15] Guo Ting and Sheng Bin. "The Asia-Pacific Regional Economic Integration, Transnational Production Game and China's Strategic Choice" (Yatai quyu jingji yitihua boyi yu Zhongguo de zhanlue xuanze), *World Economics and Politics*, no. 10, 2014.

agreement with ASEAN. China is also in talks with Japan and South Korea in an effort to reach an ASEAN Plus Three trade agreement.

More significantly, China actively advocates the discussion and negotiation of RCEP as a new FTA that incorporates sub-agreements within its broader framework. Each country can define its own interests and requirements in order to reach a consensus with other countries. This approach intends to place the ASEAN-centred 10+1, 10+3, and 10+6 frameworks in hierarchical orders where the 10+1 FTAs serve as the foundation. Members will integrate existing commitments with regulatory provisions, and further extend and enhance the content of existing agreements.[16] As a result, RCEP not only improves bilateral economic ties between countries in the region, but also promotes regional cooperation and East Asia's economic integration.

Trade and investment facilitation

The segmentation and diversification of production, together with growing offshore outsourcing and cross-border investment, have led to surging trade in intermediate goods and in services. Better rules and regulations for trade and cross-border investment are therefore an imperative in the face of expanding global and regional value chains. These have posed new challenges for developing countries as they need to enhance their legal systems and increase their economic openness.

Much more needs to be done for China and for many of its developing neighbours. China scores better than Asia's average in most cases on trade facilitation, but lags behind countries such as Singapore, Malaysia and Hong Kong (Table 11). There are still room for improvement in areas such as appeal procedures, documentation formalities and internal border agency cooperation.

In addition, China needs to expand the coverage of its FTAs. Only a handful of the 12 existing regional trade agreements that it had signed included the so-called new trade and investment issues. Table 12 shows a summary of the items covered in three concluded agreements — namely the ASEAN FTA, China–ASEAN FTA and China–South Korea

---

[16] Ibid.

Table 11. Trade Facilitation Performance of Major Asian Countries, 2015

	CHN	HKG	IDN	MYS	SGP	VNM	Asia
Information availability	1.80	2.00	1.80	1.60	2.00	1.80	1.60
Involvement of the trade community	1.75	1.75	1.5	1.25	2.00	1.00	1.33
Advance rulings	1.43	1.71	1.14	1.43	2.00	1.57	1.01
Appeal procedures	1.13	—	1.5	1.75	2.00	1.75	1.34
Fees and Charges	1.75	1.50	1.75	1.75	1.75	1.00	1.15
Formalities (Documentation)	0.83	2.00	1.17	1.83	1.83	1.00	0.94
Formalities (Automation)	1.75	1.80	1.5	1.25	1.8	1.25	1.16
Formalities (Procedures)	1.50	1.80	1.27	1.5	1.8	1.31	1.27
Internal border agency cooperation	1.00	1.67	1.00	1.33	2.00	1.33	1.48
External border agency cooperation	1.00	1.50	1.07	0.50	0.50	0.75	1.07
Governance and impartiality	1.57	1.88	1.75	1.75	2.00	1.63	1.38

Source: OECD Trade Facilitation Indicators.

Table 12. Comparison of Multilateral FTAs Involving East Asian Countries

		ASEAN FTA	China–ASEAN FTA	China–South Korean FTA	TPP
Market access Tariff quotas	Tariff reduction	√	√	√	√
	Tariff quotas	√		√	
Non-tariff measures		√		√	
Trade facilitation	Customs procedures	√	√	√	√
	Sanitary and phytosanitary	√		√	
	Technical standard	√	√	√	√
	Mutual authentication	√	√		√
Rules of Origin		√	√	√	√
Trade remedy	Anti-dumping	√	√	√	√
	Countervailing	√		√	√
	Subsidy				√
	Safeguard measures	√			√

Table 12. (*Continued*)

		ASEAN FTA	China–ASEAN FTA	China–South Korean FTA	TPP
Trade in Services	Exceptions and reservations		√	√	√
	Market access		√	√	√
	Mutual recognition		√	√	√
	Denial of benefits clause		√	√	√
	Safeguard measures		√	√	√
Investment			√		
Government Procurement				√	√
Competition Policy				√	√
Intellectual property				√	√
E-commerce				√	√
Labour standards					√
Environmental policy				√	√
Dispute settlement		√	√	√	√
Technical cooperation			√		√
Institutional mechanisms		√			√

Sources: Sheng Bin, "In the Face of the Opportunities and Challenges of International Trade and Investment New Rules" (Yinjie guoji maoyi yu touzi xinguize de jiyu yu tiaozhan), *International Trade*, no. 2, 2014. Data on China and South Korea FTA were calculated by authors based on the Regional Trade Agreements and Preferential Trade Arrangements from the World Trade Organisation databases.

FTA — and an agreement under negotiation, the TPP. While the China–South Korea agreement had included some "second-generation" issues such as government procurement, competition policy, intellectual property, e-commerce, environmental policy and dispute settlement, it still excludes certain high-standard issues, such as investment and labour. Moreover, the agreement is still limited in its scope and specific provisions.

Chapter 2

The Internationalisation of China's Renminbi

WAN Jing*

In recent years the Chinese government has intensified its efforts to promote the internationalisation of the country's currency, the renminbi. As the economies of China and East Asia integrate further, both sides will benefit greatly from the progress of renminbi internationalisation. While there is no clear definition of currency internationalisation, a general consensus on the necessary conditions for a nation's currency to be recognised as an international currency does exist. These include (i) big enough and diversified economy with strong trade position; (ii) deep and liberalised financial market; (iii) stable and reliable macroeconomic and its policy framework; (iv) relatively open capital account; and (v) government's willingness to provide liquidity to foreign countries.

Generally currency internationalisation can bring a nation various benefits, such as (i) denominating in domestic currency thus reducing exchange risks and boosting export; (ii) acquiring domestic liquidity by issuing bonds to foreign countries; (iii) getting seigniorage from a much larger scale; and (iv) making domestic financial intermediaries

---

* WAN Jing is Assistant Professor, College of Management and Economics, Tianjin University.

more influential around the world. According to 'The report of Renminbi internationalisation 2015'[1] by China's central bank, the first and the fourth are most attractive to Chinese authorities at present.

Renminbi internationalisation is a very broad and profound goal for China, which requires substantial undertaking in various major sectors of the entire financial system. As suggested by the report, it depends on (i) the degree of interest rate liberalisation, (ii) the maturity of a multi-layer capital market, (iii) free convertibility of renminbi and (iv) further opening up of the capital account. While the tasks are difficult, the government has exerted great efforts and made considerable achievement from 2013 to 2015; its efforts have attained some positive results, such as meeting some of the aforementioned standards and made many accomplishments.

One example is the launch of the Shanghai-Hong Kong stock market connect scheme in 2014 aimed at observing market reaction and testing the feasibility to further open the capital market. Meanwhile, China completed its final step of interest rate liberalisation in early 2015 and has further opened up its bonds market since 2013. The decision in 2015 by the International Monetary Fund (IMF) to include the renminbi in the special drawing rights (SDR) basket is the most significant event in the process of renminbi internationalisation especially because of the satisfaction of the 'freely usable' criteria defined by the IMF.[2] Most recently the momentum is continuing as several new moves have been carried out, including China's finance ministry announcement that it will issue RMB3 billion ($458 million) of bonds in London's offshore renminbi market and Hong Kong's Stock Exchange's aim of launching the first yuan benchmark index.

China will continue to work on increasing the flexibility of renminbi exchange rate, broadening the stock connect scheme by establishing the

---

[1] "The Report of Renminbi Internationalisation 2015", People's Bank of China, June 2015.
[2] The 'freely usable' criteria include meeting the standards in major areas, such as cross border payment, international foreign reserves, international liabilities and foreign exchange trading.

bridge between Shenzhen and Hong Kong, and enhancing the international interaction in the bonds market and so on, while opening the property market may still be too early to discuss.

The rest of this chapter is organised as follows. Section 2 illustrates China's overall endeavours towards renminbi internationalisation. Section 3 particularly analyses the significance of renminbi joining the SDR basket. Section 4 gives concluding remarks.

Recent Development and China's New Endeavours

Renminbi internationalisation is a long difficult process. We can examine the development from several aspects, such as interest liberalisation, changes in the management of exchange rate and capital account liberalisation. There has been much new progress in all three areas since 2013, which we will discuss separately.

Interest rate liberalisation

Interest rate liberalisation started nearly two decades ago, in 1996. As is shown (Table 1), considerable progress has since been made in areas including removal of the lower limit of renminbi deposit rates in 2004, removal of the lending rate floor 2013 and so on. In October 2015, the final barrier, the upper limit of deposit rates was removed. China's central bank also claims that it will continue improving the regulatory mechanism of interest rate liberalisation, enhancing the supervision on the interest rate system and increasing the transmission efficiency of monetary policy. Obviously, domestic interest rates deregulation will create a more competitive business environment, thus promoting more efficient capital allocation. Table 1 shows the timeline of China's interest rate liberalisation.

More flexible renminbi exchange rate regime

Exchange rate liberalisation is considered riskier compared with interest liberalisation, hence the more cautious approach of the government.

Table 1. China's Interest Rate Liberalisation Timeline

	Capital Market Interest Rate	Renminbi Lending Rates	Renminbi Deposit Rates
1996	Interbank offered rate becomes fully market-based		
1997	Interbank bond repo rate becomes fully market-based		
1998	China Development Bank issues the first market-priced policy bonds	The People's Bank of China (PBOC) introduces a floating range of lending rates by lifting the upper bound on lending rates gradually	
1999	Government bonds issued through open bid	Floating range of lending rates is set at 0.9×, 1.1× for large enterprises, and 0.9×, 1.3× for SMEs	
2004 (28 Oct)		Upper limit of lending rates removed	Lower limit of renminbi deposit rates removed
2006		Lower limit of mortgage loan rate set at 0.85× benchmark	
2008	China enacts a $580 billion rescue package in response to the global financial crisis		
2010–2011	The PBOC raises bank reserve requirement ratios for the 12th time		
2012		Lower limit of lending rate lowered to 0.8× benchmark in June, then 0.7× benchmark in July	Upper limit of deposit rates raised to 1.1× benchmark

2013 (19 July)	• Lending rate floor removed • Allow nine commercial banks to submit the lending rate for their best clients each day to set the prime rate • Allow the issuance of large negotiable certificates of deposit on the interbank market
2014 (22 Nov)	• Upper limit of deposit rates raised to 1.2× benchmark
2015 (1 Mar)	• Upper limit of deposit rates raised to 1.3× benchmark
(10 May)	• Upper limit of deposit rates raised to 1.5× benchmark
(2 Jun)	• Allow the issuance of large-denomination, floating-rate tradeable certificates of deposit (CDs) to individuals and companies
(24 Oct)	• Upper limit of the deposit rates removed

Source: The People's Bank of China, *A Report on the Steady Progress Made on Interest Rate Liberalisation Reforms* (January 2005), and various notices issued by The People's Bank of China.

China's sudden devaluation of its currency on 11 August 2015, allowing it to fall sharply against the US dollar by almost two per cent , was indicative of the accelerating speed of the exchange rate reform. The fluctuation of the renminbi has obviously amplified since, showing that market begins to play a more important role.

On 26 May 2015, IMF said the yuan was no longer undervalued. A month thereafter on 27 June 2015, the central bank said it would continue to push ahead with reforms of the exchange rate formation mechanism. On 11 August 2015, daily central parity rates reported to the China Foreign Exchange Trade System before the opening of the market were to be based on the closing rate of the inter-bank foreign exchange market on the previous day, supply and demand in the market, and price movements of major currencies. This is a big step towards a more flexible and more marketised exchange rate regime. On the same day, the central parity rate of the yuan against the US dollar weakened sharply by 1,136 basis points to 6.2298. A day later, the IMF described the previous day's policy change as "a welcome step" that allows market forces to have a greater role in determining the exchange rate and the renminbi-US dollar rate declined by 1,008 basis points to 6.3306.

Capital account liberalisation

Capital account liberalisation is a key step in the process of a currency's internationalisation. "The report of Renminbi internationalisation 2015" suggests the necessity of further opening up the capital accounts. The People's Bank of China (PBoC) has seriously considered opening capital account five years ago. Another report titled, 'Conditions for accelerating capital account opening' was released in February 2012[3] by a central bank research team, stating prospects for capital account liberalisation and suggesting that the conditions for capital account liberalisation are basically ready.

---
[3] <http://finance.people.com.cn/bank/GB/17224886.html> (last accessed 5 July 2016).

Table 2. Three-stage Medium-term Action Plan for Capital Account Opening

Time Span	Plan Contents
2012–2015	Relaxing control of investment directly related to trade and encouraging Chinese enterprises to increase overseas foreign direct investment
2015–2017	Relaxing trade-related commercial credit control and pushing forward renminbi internationalisation
2017–2022	Strengthening financial sector development, opening channels for credit to flow in and out of China, opening the property, stock and bond markets, and moving from quantity-based to price-based approaches to monetary management

Source: Research Group of Department of Investigation and Statistics of the People's Bank of China, "Woguo jiakuai ziben zhanghu kaifang de jiben tiaojian chengshu" (China Is Almost Ready for Accelerating Its Financial Market Opening), *China Finance* (*Zhongguo jinrong*), vol. 5, 2012.

According to the 2012 report, China was already in a relatively good position to move ahead with capital account liberalisation, based on its economic performance before 2012, and listed a three-stage medium-term action plan (Table 2).

Many accomplishments have been achieved according to the schedule for the last three to four years, which prove that the pace of capital account liberalisation has indeed accelerated.

Stock market opening: The Shanghai-Hong Kong Stock Connect scheme

Both the Shanghai-Hong Kong Stock Connect and the Shenzhen-Hong Kong Connect are China's endeavours to directly open its capital market. China also hoped to join global stock index. Opening up China's capital markets to the world is one of the centrepieces of a package to overhaul the financial market announced by President Xi Jinping in November 2014.[4] The scheme broadens the channel for offshore renminbi investment and enormously increases the volume of cross-border renminbi usage because overseas investors need to acquire

---
[4] <http://www.thepaper.cn/newsDetail_forward_1276733> (last accessed 5 July 2016).

offshore renminbi before they can invest in China's domestic A-share market. As such, renminbi's global status will be strengthened.

The scheme is a substantial step forward for capital market's further opening up and renminbi internationalisation. According to data from the Society for Worldwide Interbank Financial Telecommunication (SWIFT), a global transaction service, renminbi now ranks seventh in global payment currencies.[5] This is consistent with views expressed by Zhou Xiaochuan, the former governor of the People's Bank of China, who stated that the Stock Connect aims to encourage investment in both directions, hoping to not only consolidate Hong Kong's position as a financial centre, but also help improve the mechanisms of the Mainland's capital market.[6]

Capital restrictions have isolated China's capital markets. Outward portfolio investment (domestic investment in foreign securities) amounted to just three per cent of China's gross domestic product (GDP), compared to 49% for the United States. The contrast is even starker for inward portfolio investment (foreign investment in domestic securities): four per cent of GDP in China as opposed to 86% in the United States. There is a clear need for China to open up its capital market.

Li Xiaojia, chief executive as well as executive director of Hong Kong Exchanges and Clearing Ltd, suggested that the ongoing Stock Connect schemes can help renminbi internationalisation to gain some experiences on renminbi circulation system first.[7] Officials hailed the pilot programme as a major institutional innovation in capital markets, while showing their concern on the opening-up of the capital account. The potential outflow of a huge amount of capital will have great impact on the exchange rate of renminbi, domestic interest rate and asset pricing of the Mainland once the capital account is open.

---

[5] Research report, from SWIFT (member-owned cooperative providing the communications platform, products and services).
[6] Zhou Xiaochuan, "Broadening the Fluctuation Range of Interest Rate of Renminbi Deposit".
[7] Li Xiaojia concluded that investment through the Stock Connect by using renminbi helps to develop the circulation system of the renminbi, which offers a thorough grounding for renminbi internationalisation before it begins to take shape.

The Stock Connect scheme provides China with an opportunity to gain useful experiences that promote China's capital market and raise its international reach. The primary task of the Stock Connect scheme is to consider how these unprecedented experiences can be transplanted if the scheme proves successful. It signifies the next stage in the opening up of China's capital markets and is very likely to accelerate renminbi internationalisation.

Further opening up of the bonds market

As the roaring stock market has grabbed all the attention, the public rarely noticed that a big portion of China's vast capital market has been quietly opened to foreign investors at a record pace. For the first half of 2015, the central bank accelerated approvals for overseas participants in the country's debt market. The central bank has allowed a further 32 foreign institutional investors in the first half of 2015 to trade in the $6.1 trillion interbank bond market. Together with 34 approvals in all of 2014, it brought the total number of approved foreign investors to 152 as of April 2015, not counting sovereign-wealth funds and central banks.

For interbank market participants, foreign investors account for around 38.6%, domestic commercial banks 52.8% and the rest are made up by domestic insurance companies. In view of the big proportion of foreign investors and the fact that the Chinese government has already removed its tight control of domestic interest rate, the interbank bond market may become more volatile in the future. Overseas fund managers held RMB713 billion ($115 billion) of domestic Chinese bonds, according to central bank data in mid 2016. That was more than the RMB601 billion as of May 2015 held in onshore stocks, notwithstanding that the stock market attracted the most public attention. China's acceleration of approval granting is very meaningful because its currency would become more widely held abroad, which certainly helps turn renminbi into a global reserve currency. In the future, bringing more foreign investors into its bond market will help China overcome economic downturn, providing some stability by offsetting the capital outflow.

The sudden acceleration in the pace of allowing investors into the interbank bond market is indeed central bank's attempt to offset the capital flowing out of China. The outflow of capital has been hitting record since the second quarter of 2015. This is one of the clear signs that speculators are transferring money out of China and companies are becoming more cautious about holding renminbi, as China's economy has slowed and expectations on renminbi is not so optimistic.

Opening up the interbank bond market and giving foreign investors another place to park their cash in low-risk government bonds definitely help China attain its aim of having the yuan included in the IMF's elite basket of currencies that make up its emergency lending reserves — the SDR basket, which was achieved at the end of 2015. Now that the Chinese currency is included in the IMF's basket of reserve currencies, foreign investors could hold $744 billion to $1.1 trillion of all Chinese onshore bonds in 2020, according to estimations of some foreign investment banks.

Recent development in other areas

Renminbi's internationalisation is not confined to the aforementioned four aspects. Recently there are some progress in other areas that help consolidate the outside environment for renminbi to go further. One example is the development of renminbi's offshore market. In May 2016, the ministry of finance of China announced that it will issue RMB3 billion ($458 million) of bonds in London's offshore renminbi market to test foreign investors' appetite for Chinese assets amid concerns about the currency's depreciation and capital outflow. Providing foreign investors with a deep and liquid pool of high-quality renminbi assets is crucial to China's goal of boosting international use of its currency. Renminbi deposits have accumulated in offshore centres including Hong Kong, London, Singapore and Frankfurt at a significant level over the years, but the supply of offshore renminbi financial assets has always lagged behind.

Almost at the same time, Hong Kong's stock exchange claims it is going to create a benchmark index for the yuan to try to spur offshore trading of the Chinese currency, which has suffered setbacks as China slowly liberalises the flow of money in and out of the Mainland. These two drastic moves are related and supplementary to each other, enhancing the international power of renminbi and marking a new step in opening up China's capital account.

The process of transforming China's quantitative-based monetary policy framework to a price-based one has also been accelerated as interest rate liberalisation has been completed and the reforms on bonds market have helped improve the yields comprehensively.

The achievements mentioned so far all bring broader benefits to mainland China by improving the mechanism of its money and capital market; in the long run they will enhance the usage of cross-border renminbi, paving the way for renminbi internationalisation and gathering experiences for the opening up of its capital market. Joining SDR is the most significant event in the process of renminbi internationalisation.

Joining SDR Basket

After so many years of efforts, on 30 November 2015, the most prominent accomplishment of the reform of the exchange rate so far in China was fulfilled: The IMF included Chinese yuan in the current SDR basket effective 1 October 2016. China has been looking forward to the result since 2009, and the journey towards this goal has not been easy as there are still many dissenting voices which question the meaning, significance and impact of the inclusion.

Function of SDR

SDRs are supplementary foreign exchange reserve assets defined and managed by the IMF. Their value is based on a basket of key international currencies reviewed by the IMF. SDRs per se are not technically a currency. SDRs held by IMF member countries represent a claim to currency which may be exchanged when needed. To put it differently, it gives IMF member countries who hold it the right to obtain any of the currencies in the basket to meet balance-of-payments needs. As they can only be exchanged for US dollars, euro, pounds sterling, Japanese yen or the new comer, Chinese yuan, SDRs may actually represent a potential claim on IMF member countries' non-gold foreign exchange reserves.

The IMF once issued a report in 2011 indicating that the current role of the SDR is insignificant.[8] One reason for SDRs' insignificant role could be the requirement to exchange it into a currency before use, which means SDRs as foreign reserves do not meet the basic functions of foreign exchange reserves.[9] Due to this fact, developed countries, which hold the most SDRs, are unlikely to use them for any purpose. The IMF labelled the SDR as an "imperfect reserve asset".

As of September 2015, there was an equivalent of about US$280 billion in SDRs created and allocated to IMF members. SDRs are allocated to IMF member countries only. Therefore private parties do not hold or use them. During the financial crisis of 2009, SDR had indeed made contributions in providing liquidity to the global economic system as the IMF allocated an additional $283 billion of SDR[10] to its member countries to enrich their official reserves.

The inclusion of renminbi in SDR basket

The current requirements adopted for SDR basket inclusion date back to the year 2000. To qualify, a currency has to meet two criteria, the first being that its exports of goods and services during the five-year period ending 12 months before the effective date of the revision have the largest value, or 'export requirement' for short. It aims to ensure currencies that qualify for the basket are those issued by

---

[8] IMF report, 'Enhancing International Monetary Stability — A Role for the SDR?' 7 January 2011.
[9] Basic functions of foreign exchange reserves, such as market intervention and liquidity provision, as well as some less prosaic ones, such as maintaining export competitiveness via favourable exchange rates, cannot be accomplished directly using SDRs.
[10] <http://www.imf.org/external/pubs/ft/survey/so/2009/POL082809A.htm> (last accessed 13 January 2015).

members or monetary unions that play a central role in the global economy. This criterion has been part of the SDR methodology since the 1970s.

The second requirement for currencies in the SDR basket to be also freely usable was incorporated in 2000 to formally reflect the importance of financial transactions for the purposes of valuing the SDR basket. 'Freely usable' refers to (i) being widely used to make payments for international transactions and (ii) being widely traded in the principal exchange markets. IMF clearly states that the concept of a freely usable currency concerns the actual international use and trading of currencies, and is distinct from whether a currency is either freely floating or fully convertible. In other words, the facts are that the renminbi is not yet fully convertible as China still imposes capital controls and the related renminbi exchange rate mechanism shall not be considered obstacles to the renminbi's path to the SDRs.

Over the course of the 2008 financial crisis, the IMF progressively relaxed its stance on "free-market" principles such as its guidance against using capital controls, which makes Chinese yuan easier to meet the second requirement. In 2010, when reviewing the SDR currencies basket, the IMF examined and analysed whether the renminbi met its requirements and the renminbi was the only currency being seriously considered at the time. China met the first criterion in 2010 as it was the world's third largest exporter of goods and services at that time. However, the IMF concluded that the renminbi had not met the second requirement of being "freely usable" and thus decided to maintain the status quo.

Global usage of the yuan has surged since the last rejection by IMF of its inclusion in the SDR in the review in 2010. Renminbi has become the fourth most-used currency in global payments, with a 2.79% share in August 2016, surpassing the yen, according to SWIFT. IMF also viewed the move of accelerating the devaluation of yuan on 11 August 2015 as part of China's efforts to further liberalise its foreign exchange rates, suggesting that the IMF had no misgivings about the yuan's joining the SDR benchmark basket. However, the widely anticipated addition of the Chinese yuan to SDR's benchmark currency

Table 3. Currency Weights, Quota and Voting Power

Nation		Currency Weights	SDR Quota	Voting Power
US (Dollar)		41.73%	17.7%	16.7%
Japan (Yen)		8.33%	6.6%	6.2%
Euro Zone	(Germany)	30.93%	6.1%	5.8%
	(France)		4.5%	4.3%
UK (Pound)		8.09%	4.5%	4.3%
China (Yuan)		10.92%	4.0%	3.8%

Source: compiled by the author based on information from IMF.

basket was deferred on 20 August 2016 by the IMF. IMF claimed that this decision was the result of responding to feedback from SDR users on the desirability of avoiding changes in the basket. IMF thought that a sufficient lead time should be given to users to adjust in the event of an addition of a new currency to the basket.

IMF decided to include Chinese yuan in the SDR basket on 30 November 2015. Weights calculated by the new formula were used to determine the amount of each of the five currencies in the new SDR basket.

Of note is the fact that renminbi's inclusion and weights are irrelevant to the SDR quota weightage or its resultant allocation of IMF voting power. For now, the renminbi has been accorded a weight of 10.9% in the SDR basket, higher than that of the Japanese yen and British pound. However, China's SDR quota is still only four per cent, with 3.8% voting power, the lowest among other countries. In contrast, the United States has the largest quota of 17.7% and 16.7% voting power, which is summarised in Table 3.

China's joining the SDR: Implications

As mentioned earlier, technically SDRs constitute an international reserve asset aiming to maintain a balance between member countries with external liabilities and those with abundant cash. In practice, they are more marginal, as countries largely rely on capital markets and hard currencies to cover their obligations. Therefore if joining SDR alone may not seem to be so significant, why the keenness on China's part? China perhaps saw it as a way to boost relations with countries like Britain. Many major economies, including the United States, Germany and Britain, had indicated their readiness to back the yuan's inclusion if it meets the IMF criteria. Supporting the yuan may boost relations between China and countries such as Britain, which has sought to make London a major yuan trading hub. IMF's decision is also a clear vote of confidence for the Chinese central bank.

On the other hand, how could the IMF or other countries benefit from the yuan's inclusion? In a 2009 speech, former People's Bank of China governor Zhou Xiaochuan said the 2008 global financial crisis underscored the risks of a global monetary system that relies on national reserve currencies.[11] Zhou argued that the SDR should take on the role of a "super-sovereign reserve currency" with its basket expanded to include currencies of all major economies because a national currency was unsuitable as a global reserve currency due to the Triffin dilemma. Both Richard Cooper, chairman of the Federal Reserve Bank of Boston from 1990 to 1992, and Ronald McKinnon, professor of economics at the Stanford University since 1961, agreed with Zhou's argument about the asymmetric situation of international currency arrangements.

As the US dollar is the de facto international money, the United States alone has an ultra-soft international borrowing constraint and is free to increase debt without devaluation risk. Meanwhile the huge US cumulative current account deficits tend to further prevent most emerging markets from international borrowing, so liquidity demand cannot be fully met in the global market as the United States has its own interest to attain.

Years after the 2008 financial crisis, globalisation through increased trade and capital flows had resulted in the existing international monetary system becoming more and more inherently fragile. IMF was well aware

---

[11] <http://chinese.wsj.com/gb/20090323/bch195226.asp> (last accessed 18 January 2016).

of the drawbacks and risks of an absence of a super-sovereign reserve money and very clear that reforms must be carried out to gradually rely less on the US dollar as the single international reserve money. Meanwhile nurturing a super-sovereign reserve money is necessary and SDR is still the most favourable choice notwithstanding the various difficulties.

China had noticed the changes within IMF and had been making its bigger plan for years. China did not expect its joining the SDR to play a big role under the existing framework of IMF; its emphasis is in the future. In other words, the vision of China's central bank is beyond the ken of the current international monetary system. What China really wants is an ongoing restructuring within IMF which brings more opportunities for SDRs to play an essential role in dealing with the underlying asymmetries. Until then, renminbi as a major currency in the basket would release more of its potential and function akin to an international money.

Winning the IMF's endorsement allows reformers within the Chinese government to argue that the shift towards a more international renminbi has begun to bear fruit. However, even though renminbi has already met the criteria and successfully joined the SDR basket, there are aspects to be improved in the future. Only by continuing to improve could China have the opportunity to increase its voting power in the IMF, a more meaningful endeavour.

Overall, renminbi's strength lies in exports, trade finance and payment. Its weakness lies in central bank holdings and the renminbi international bond market. Central bank holdings will not be problematic anymore as at least US$1 trillion of global reserves will migrate to Chinese assets if the yuan joins the IMF's reserve basket according to Standard Chartered Plc. Currently the offshore renminbi bond market size of 480 billion yuan results in a rather small share of 0.4% of the total, which suggests that the room for issuing renminbi bonds is very huge. Foreign companies' issuance of yuan-denominated securities in China, known as panda bonds, could exceed US$50 billion in the next five years according to the World Bank's International Finance Corp.[12]

---

[12] <http://www.thestar.com.my/business/business-news/2015/12/03/yuan-imf-win-awakens-sleepy-panda-bond-market/?style=biz> (last accessed 15 June 2016).

Conclusion

Since 2012, China had gone through several meaningful reforms in the financial sector that significantly support the progress of renminbi internationalisation; however, China now faces uncertainty from both outside and inside, which will hinder the ongoing process to a large extent.

Internationally, worldwide slowdown of the world economy leads to conflicts within and among countries; the United States had stopped its Quantitative Easing (QE) in October 2014 and is in a cycle of increasing its interest rate which strengthens US dollar even stronger, while other countries are still injecting liquidity into their markets through QE, which results in worldwide monetary policy divergence. Domestically, the economic fundamentals in China are not optimistic and the financial sector is still immature and under-regulated. China's central bank has attempted to stick to its policy guidelines of easy monetary policy domestically and stable exchange rate internationally. However, when in a conflict, such as under current uncertain environment of both domestic (the deleveraging in real estate sector and so on) and international (the ongoing trade war with the United States) economy, China as a big economy will most probably choose economic stability and monetary policy independence over the stabilisation of exchange rate regime as its best policy combination. Therefore a more volatile depreciation process of renminbi is foreseeable and the pace of renminbi expansion might not be as fast as in previous years.

Meanwhile with the international environment becoming more unstable and unpredictable, risks level will be raised accordingly. Understandably, China as well as the rest of the world will hold a rather cautious attitude. IMF has warned that accelerating the capital account opening could lead to a massive outflow of money from China if not handled properly. As early as July 2013, IMF had said that financial-sector liberalisation, especially for its interest rates and currency, is necessary to keep China growing healthily over the coming decades. Notably, IMF has shown genuine concern over whether China is ready for significant capital-account liberalisation, which is an indispensable part of renminbi internationalisation. Therefore, renminbi internationalisation is a goal that could only be reached by very cautious footsteps.

China's economic integration with Asia will benefit from and test the degree of the renminbi internationalisation. In this learning-by-doing process, China can gain valuable experiences from the communication and interaction with other Asian countries as a starting point, especially in the aspects of how to better improve trade and transactions with renminbi services and so on in order to better support China's long-term greater plan of the Belt and Road Initiative. With so many challenges and uncertainties ahead, the pace of renminbi internationalisation should be carefully designed to complement China's other aims.

Chapter 3

The Internationalisation of Chinese Enterprises

CHEN Chien-Hsun*

After China's implementation of economic reforms in 1978, economic activities of all kinds started to take off. In particular, the Chinese government developed foreign trade to acquire foreign technology. By the late 1980s, the Chinese government had not only continued the process of institutional transformation and pushed to attract foreign capital, technology and management experience, but also encouraged the country's enterprises to invest overseas.[1] This was immediately followed by 15 years of negotiation for the World Trade Organisation (WTO) accession. In 2000, China launched a "go global" (*zou chuqu*) strategy, strongly supporting and encouraging Chinese firms with competitive advantage to venture abroad. This strategy creates areas of comparative advantage for Chinese firms by promoting multinational operations, and actively developing and utilising overseas resources.

---

* CHEN Chien-Hsun is an Advisor with the Regional Development Study Center at Chung-Hua Institution for Economic Research, Taipei, Taiwan.
[1] John Wong and Sarah Chan, "China's Outward Direct Investment: Expanding Worldwide", *China: An International Journal*, vol. 1, no. 2, 2003, pp. 273–301.

With the opening up of China and strengthening of its domestic enterprises, an increasing number of Chinese firms have ventured to other countries. From the Chinese government's perspective, the increase in China's foreign direct investment (FDI) outflow has enhanced its political and economic leverage.[2] China's central government policies and regulations have played a critical role in its overseas investment.[3] The 12th Five-Year Programme (2011–2015) emphasised the importance of the "go global" strategy and projected the outward FDI to increase at an annual rate of 17% and hit US$150 billion by 2015.[4] In November 2013, China unveiled an aggressive reform package after the Third Plenum of the 18th Communist Party of China's Central Committee. The package included signing of more bilateral and multilateral investment agreements to boost China's overseas investment.[5]

After weathering the 1997 Asian financial crisis, China joined the WTO in 2001. China's accession to the WTO followed the tide of globalisation and it gradually grew in strength in the international arena, ahead of many developing countries. Although the United States subprime crisis triggered a global financial crisis in 2008, which slowed global economic growth, China achieved 10.4% economic growth in

---

[2] Since 2010, China's implementation of government-sponsored investment activities has escalated. Charles Wolf Jr., Wang Xiao and Eric Warner, *China's Foreign Aid and Government-Sponsored Investment Activities: Scale, Content, Destinations, and Implications*, California, RAND Corporation, 2013.

[3] China's government support and well-developed host country institutions enhanced FDI entry into a host country. Lu Jiangyong, Liu Xiaohui, Mike Wright and Igor Filatotchev, "International Experience and FDI Location Choices of Chinese Firms: The Moderating Effects of Home Country Government Support and Host Country Institutions", *Journal of International Business Studies*, vol. 45, no. 4, 2014, pp. 428–449.

[4] "Chinese Outbound Foreign Direct Investment Faces Rigorous Scrutiny", *China Briefing*, at <http://www.china-briefing.com/news/2012/12/31/chinese-outbound-foreign-direct-investment-faces-rigorous-scrutiny-2.html> (accessed 16 August 2013).

[5] "Decision of the Central Committee of the Communist Party of China on Some Major Issues Concerning Comprehensively Deepening the Reform", *China Daily*, 16 November 2013.

2010 and 7.7% in 2013. It has become an economic power that led in the global economic recovery.

In 2001, China's outward foreign direct investment (OFDI) totalled US$6.9 billion. Nevertheless, by the end of 2014, its OFDI reached US$123.12 billion, registering US$882.64 billion in total overseas investments. Indeed, Chinese multinational companies are large in size. For example, China International Trading and Investment Corporation (CITIC Group), with US$71.5 billion in foreign assets, was the largest overseas investor in 2011. China Ocean Shipping (Group) Company was the second-largest overseas investor with US$40.4 billion in foreign assets, followed by China National Offshore Oil Corporation with US$29.8 billion, China National Petroleum Corporation with US$17.0 billion, and Sinochem Group with US$13.1billion in foreign assets.[6] In 2014, 95 Chinese companies or roughly 19.0% of them were ranked among the world's 500 largest companies.[7]

Chinese multinational companies have played an important role in overseas investment activities. China was once an insignificant OFDI country, but has progressed to become an important source of global investment. According to the United Nations Conference on Trade and Development, China was ranked the third-largest source of global outward FDI in 2014 for three consecutive years. In the foreseeable future, China's outward FDI is likely to continue in upward swing.

FDI trends have shown that OFDI will have a profound effect on the home or host country's economy. The location choice and OFDI pattern are still the main determining factors of OFDI. As shown in Table 1, the share of China's OFDI is far higher in Asia than in other regions during the 2005–2014 period. Although the share of China's OFDI in Asia was lower than that in Latin America in 2005 and 2006,

---

[6] United Nations Conference on Trade and Development (UNCTAD), *World Investment Report 2013*, at <http://unctad.org/en/PublicationsLibrary/wir2013_en.pdf> (accessed 5 April 2016).
[7] Ministry of Commerce of China, at <http://www.mofcom.gov.cn> (accessed 5 April 2016).

Table 1. Geographical Pattern of China's OFDI (Flow), 2005–2014 (%)

	2005	2006	2007	2008	2009	2010	2011	2012	2013	2014
Asia	36.57	43.46	62.60	77.89	71.48	65.24	60.94	73.78	70.11	69.03
Hong Kong	27.89	39.30	51.81	69.12	62.98	55.96	47.76	58.36	58.25	57.56
Indonesia	0.10	0.32	0.37	0.31	0.40	0.29	0.79	1.55	1.45	1.03
Japan	0.14	0.22	0.15	0.10	0.15	0.49	0.20	0.24	0.40	0.32
Macao	0.07	−0.24	0.18	1.15	0.81	0.14	0.27	0.02	0.37	0.48
Singapore	0.17	0.75	1.50	2.77	2.50	1.63	4.38	1.73	1.88	2.29
Republic of Korea	4.80	0.15	0.21	0.17	0.47	−1.05	0.46	1.07	0.25	0.45
Thailand	0.04	0.09	0.29	0.08	0.09	1.02	0.31	0.55	0.70	0.68
Vietnam	0.17	0.25	0.42	0.21	0.20	0.44	0.25	0.40	0.45	0.27
Africa	3.19	2.95	5.94	9.82	2.55	3.07	4.25	2.87	3.13	2.60
Algeria	0.69	0.56	0.55	0.08	0.40	0.27	0.15	0.28	0.18	0.54
Sudan	0.74	0.29	0.25	−0.11	0.03	0.04	1.22	0.00	0.13	0.14
Nigeria	0.43	0.38	1.47	0.29	0.30	0.27	0.26	0.38	0.19	0.16
South Africa	0.39	0.23	1.71	8.60	0.07	0.60	−0.02	−0.93	−0.08	0.03
Europe	3.23	3.39	5.81	1.57	5.93	9.82	11.05	8.01	5.52	8.80
UK	0.20	0.20	2.14	0.03	0.34	0.48	1.90	3.16	1.32	1.22
Germany	1.05	0.44	0.90	0.33	0.32	0.60	0.69	0.91	0.84	1.17

France	0.05	0.03	0.04	0.06	0.08	0.04	4.66	0.18	0.24	0.33
Russia	1.66	2.56	1.80	0.71	0.62	0.83	0.96	0.89	0.95	0.51
Latin America	52.74	48.03	18.50	6.58	12.96	15.31	15.99	7.03	13.31	8.57
Brazil	0.12	0.06	0.19	0.04	0.21	0.71	0.17	0.22	0.29	0.59
Chile	0.01	0.04	0.01	0.00	0.01	0.05	0.02	0.03	0.01	0.01
Peru	0.00	0.03	0.03	0.04	0.10	0.20	0.29	−0.06	0.11	0.04
Mexico	0.03	0.02	0.06	0.01	0.00	0.04	0.06	0.11	0.05	0.11
Venezuela	0.06	0.10	0.26	0.02	0.20	0.14	0.11	1.76	0.39	0.09
Cayman Islands	42.11	44.42	9.82	2.73	9.49	5.08	6.61	0.94	8.58	3.40
British Virgin Islands	10.00	3.05	7.08	3.76	2.85	8.89	8.32	2.55	2.99	3.71
North America	2.62	1.46	4.25	0.65	2.69	3.81	3.32	5.56	4.54	7.48
Canada	0.26	0.20	3.90	0.01	1.08	1.66	0.74	0.91	0.94	0.73
USA	1.89	1.12	0.74	0.83	1.61	1.90	2.43	4.61	3.59	6.17
Oceania	1.65	0.72	2.91	3.49	4.39	2.75	4.44	2.75	3.39	3.52
Australia	1.57	0.50	2.01	3.38	4.31	2.47	4.24	2.47	3.21	3.29
New Zealand	0.03	0.02	−0.01	0.01	0.02	0.09	0.04	0.11	0.18	0.20

Sources: Ministry of Commerce of the People's Republic of China, *China Commerce Yearbook*, 2015; and National Bureau of Statistics of China, *China Statistical Yearbook*, 2006–2015, China Statistics Press.

the share in the Asian region rose to 78% in 2008 before falling to 69.03% in 2014.

In reality, the growth in Latin America was largely derived from increased investment in the Cayman Islands and the British Virgin Islands. Their tax haven status has made them important vehicles for cross-investment activity by corporations all over the world. It can be reasonably assumed that almost all of the apparent investment in the Cayman Islands and the British Virgin Islands represents investment in other countries in reality. In 2011, experiments with the use of renminbi in OFDI were permitted by the Chinese government, reflecting the progressive internationalisation of China's currency.[8]

The Importance of State-owned Enterprises

By the end of 2014, the regional distribution of Chinese overseas enterprises was centred in Asia and Europe, accounting for 54.5% and 13.8% of the total number of firms, respectively. The African region, North America, Latin America and Oceania accounted for 11.6%, 12%, 5% and 3.1% of the total, respectively. State-owned enterprises still constitute the majority of China's OFDI. Unlike those in developed countries such as the European nations, the United States and Japan, China's overseas investment is dominated by state-owned enterprises whose overseas investment activities have formed a comprehensive system for the division of labour based on the industrial development structure in the home country.

As stated in the *2014 Statistical Bulletin of China's Outward Foreign Direct Investment*, by 2014, Chinese overseas firms established in the Asia region numbered about 16,955, accounting for 57.1% of the total, mainly in Hong Kong, Japan, the United Arab Emirates, Singapore and Korea, which are regions with relatively high per capita income. In Europe, 3,330 overseas firms were established, accounting

---

[8] "China Further Expands the Use of RMB through Cross-border Foreign Direct Investment", 15 November 2011, at <http://www.lexology.com/library/detail.aspx?g=e06a5374-8dc5-46e7-a17f-fcf60f5df5c6> (accessed 17 August 2013).

for 11.2% of the total, mainly in Russia, Germany, England, Italy, the Netherlands and France.

Hong Kong has historically been the favoured host destination of Chinese round-tripping OFDI as there are incentives for Chinese companies to comply with the "foreign-owned enterprises" (FOE) status. Many Chinese firms invest in Hong Kong to transform their identity, obtain FOE status and invest in China in a different identity.[9] To obtain hard evidence of the actual figure of round-tripping is not easy. The estimate for round-tripping FDI from Hong Kong to China is probably in the range of 23% to 50% (Table 2).

By the end of 2014, state-owned enterprises accounted for 53.6% of total OFDI stock and limited liability companies made up 32.22%, while private enterprises and foreign-invested enterprises only

Table 2. Estimation of Round-Tripping Investment from China (%)

Literature	Estimation Result, %	Sample Period
Lardy, 1995	25	1993
Harrod and Lall, 1993	25	1993
Huang, 1998	Low Scenario, 23	1993
	Middle Scenario, 36	
	High Scenario, 49	
Bhaskaran, 2003	25	2003
Subramanian, 2002	50*	2002
World Bank, 2002	50*	2002
Xiao, 2004	40, between 30 and 50	1982–2003

Note: *Percentage of FDI from Hong Kong to China.

Source: Li Zhongmin, *How Foreign Direct Investment Promotes Development: The Case of the People's Republic of China's Inward and Outward FDI*, ADB Economics Working Paper Series no. 340, Asian Development Bank, 2013.

---

[9] Randall Morck and Bernard Yin Yeung and Zhao Minyuan, "Perspectives on China's Outward Foreign Direct Investment", *Journal of International Business Studies*, vol. 39, no. 3, 2008, pp. 337–350.

constituted 1.6% and 1.2%, respectively.[10] Although geographical proximity or economic integration could reduce trade costs, China still has investments in distant regions such as the Americas and Africa.

The majority of Chinese enterprises involved in transnational operations are state-owned enterprises, which are under the extensive control of the government. This is partly because the tolerance level of state-owned enterprises for political risks is higher than that of private enterprises. Indeed, political and diplomatic motivations are still important determinants of China's overseas investment decisions.[11] China hopes to make use of overseas investment to enhance its international economic and political influence.

In recent years, China has become the factory of the world and a low-cost production base for multinational companies (MNCs) for further export to third countries. China's low-cost advantages however could be replaced by other countries (such as Vietnam) with even greater advantages in terms of cost. China's MNCs are likely to follow the lead of other developed countries by capitalising on their own technological advantages and establishing factories in nearby or distant countries before exporting their products to a third country. These third-country effects could affect China's OFDI in these countries.[12] Nevertheless, Chinese OFDI has a competitive advantage in host countries with weak institutions.[13] Compared with companies of

---

[10] Ministry of Commerce of the PRC, at <http://www.mofcom.gov.cn> (accessed 31 March 2016).

[11] Sumon Kumar Bhaumik and Catherine Yap Co, "China's Economic Cooperation Related Investment: An Investigation of Its Direction and Some Implications for Outward Investment", *China Economic Review*, vol. 22, no. 1, 2011, pp. 75–87; Alessia A. Amighinia, Roberta Rabellottic and Marco Sanfilippo, "Do Chinese State-owned and Private Enterprises Differ in Their Internationalisation Strategies?", *China Economic Review*, vol. 27, 2013, pp. 312–325.

[12] Harry Garretsen and Jolanda Peeters, "FDI and the Relevance of Spatial Linkages: Do Third Country Effects Matter for Dutch FDI?" *Review of World Economics*, vol. 145, no. 2, 2009, pp. 319–338.

[13] Cheung Yin-Wong and Qian Xingwang, "The Empirics of China's Outward Direct Investment", *Pacific Economic Review*, vol. 14, no. 3, 2009, pp. 312–341; Ivar Kolstad and

developed countries, Chinese firms have abundant experience in dealing with difficult business environments and complex principal and subordinate relationships that benefit both individuals and institutions in a non-transparent political system.[14]

The Business Models of Chinese Enterprises

With liberalisation and the strengthening of Chinese business enterprises, more and more Chinese firms have begun to consider investing overseas. The exact form that overseas investment takes depends on the capabilities of the firm, the industry in which it belongs and the strategy that it adopts.

Establishing overseas marketing and distribution channels

Establishing international distribution and sales network is one such model for firms that invest overseas to market their goods directly in other countries and boost their earnings performance. The overseas investment undertaken by the 999 Group, China's leading pharmaceutical manufacturer, is an example of this model. The 999 Group's manufacturing facilities and research and development (R&D) centres are all located in China, whereas its overseas subsidiaries focus on marketing and sales. Since 1992, the 999 Group has established sales companies in over a dozen countries/regions, including Hong Kong, Russia, Malaysia, Germany and the United States; these sales companies play a very important role in promoting the sale of 999 Group products in overseas markets. Other companies that have adopted this model for their overseas investment activities include Fuyao Group, Tiens Group, Sinochem Group and China Technology Group.

Arne Wiig, "What Determines Chinese Outward FDI?", *Journal of World Business*, vol. 47, no. 1, 2012, pp. 26–34.
[14] Henry Wai-chung Yeung and Liu Weidong, "Globalizing China: The Rise of Mainland Firms in the Global Economy", *Eurasian Geography and Economics*, vol. 49, no. 1, 2008, pp. 57–86.

The main advantage of this model is that a firm can expand the scale of its exports directly and access market information more effectively. If a company's production, purchasing and R&D functions are still located in China, it is likely to be affected by trade barriers in its overseas markets.[15]

Offshore processing

The term "offshore processing" is used to refer to a situation whereby a company establishes an offshore production facility or facilities to boost exports of production equipment, technology, materials and components produced in the company's home country. As offshore processing is ideally suited to China's economy that undergoes transformation currently, it has emerged as an important model for Chinese enterprises venturing overseas over the last few years. Most of the firms that have adopted this model are in industries such as textile, home appliances, light industry or machinery manufacturing, which are characterised by mature technologies and overcapacity.

For example, in the mid-1990s, China's textile industry faced a shrinking domestic market, severe overcapacity and a host of trade barriers (in the form of export quotas) in international markets. China Worldbest Group responded to this situation by establishing offshore processing facilities in Mexico, Canada and Thailand, thereby exploiting country-of-origin rules to develop overseas markets.[16]

Overseas investments undertaken by Konka Group, Gree Group and Chunlan Group have also followed this model, which helps to drive export growth while speeding up the transformation of China's industrial structure.

Brand development in overseas markets

For Chinese companies that already possess strong brands, brand development in overseas markets by modes of joint ventures, franchising

---

[15] Peter J. Buckley, *Foreign Direct Investment, China and the World Economy*, New York, Palgrave Macmillian, 2010.

[16] China Worldbest Group, at <http://www.worldbest-cn.com> (accessed 17 August 2013).

or chain store operations is a model that they can capitalise on to develop overseas market. One such success story is Tong Ren Tang, a company headquartered in Beijing with a history of over 330 years.[17] Today, Tong Ren Tang is a large, modern manufacturer and vendor of Chinese herbal medicines; its trademark is registered in over 50 countries and regions, and its products are sold in more than 40 countries throughout the world.

A precondition for companies to have successful outcome in this model is ownership of a strong brand and intellectual property. The fact that a vast majority of Chinese companies possess neither a strong brand nor intellectual property, this model appears to have relevance and applicability to only a handful of the Chinese firms.

Acquiring stakes in foreign companies

In the stakes acquisition in foreign companies model, Chinese companies buy voting shares in a foreign company (usually a listed company), either on the open market or by subscribing to capital increments with a view to build up a sufficiently large stake in order to exercise control over the company's management. The recent years have seen a gradual increase in the number of Chinese companies adopting this strategy.

For example, in 2001, China's Wanxiang Group acquired UAI, a company listed on the NASDAQ stock exchange in the United States.[18] Investing overseas through purchase of shares in foreign companies is a relatively inexpensive form of overseas investment as it does not impose an increase in shareholders' tax liabilities. However, a Chinese company that adopts this model has to take on the liabilities of the target company.

Outbound Mergers and Acquisitions

Chinese companies are now engaged in transnational mergers and acquisitions (M&As) to acquire technology and advanced R&D

---

[17] Tong Ren Tang, at <http://www.tongrentang.com> (accessed 17 August 2013).
[18] Wanxiang Group, at <http://www.wanxiang.com> (accessed 17 August 2013).

capabilities. As China is now the world's second-largest energy consumer, it is exploring international energy resources beyond its domestic energy supply. It is also expanding both its domestic and overseas energy markets. In 2015, China's growth in outbound M&As in terms of volume hit a record high of 40% (US$67.4 billion, 382 deals) compared to 2014 (US$55.7 billion, 274 deals).[19]

Furthermore, due to market restrictions within China, some industries that have been overproducing, such as the home electronics industry and textile industry, have to achieve economies of scale and increase profit. Given the current global economic climate, this move is necessary for such industries to survive and expand market channels. China's attempts in international business are also limited by its lack of international brands.

By cooperating with foreign companies and capitalising on the division of labour in a global production chain that uses China's cost advantages and brand advantages of foreign companies, China's products have gained greater access to international markets. Chinese companies such as Lenovo,[20] Shanghai Automotive Industry Corporation (SAIC), Haier,[21] BOE Technology Group, TCL, China Petrochemical Corporation, China Three Gorges Corporation, China Investment Corporation,[22] China Petroleum & Chemical Corporation, Dalian Wanda Group Corporation Ltd, Sinopec International Petroleum Exploration and Production Corporation and China National Offshore Oil Corp (CNOOC) have in recent years begun to engage in a series of M&As in Western countries.

These initiatives have set the milestones for Chinese enterprises targeting foreign companies. However, not all M&A deals were sealed.[23]

---

[19] David Brown, *PwC M&A 2015 Review and 2016 Outlook*, at <http://www.pwccn.com> (accessed 5 April 2016).
[20] Lenovo Group acquired IBM's personal computer division in 2005.
[21] Haier's first overseas investment in the United States was in 1999.
[22] China Investment Corporation purchased 8.7% of Thames Water, the United Kingdom's largest water company, in 2012.
[23] Due to a political backlash, CNOOC failed to acquire US-based oil and gas producer Unocal in 2005.

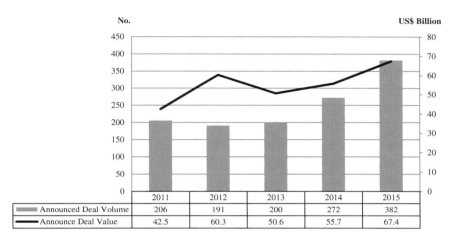

Figure 1. China Mainland Outbound Deals from 2011 to 2015
Source: David Brown, *PwC M&A 2015 Review and 2016 Outlook*, at <http://www.pwccn.com> (accessed 5 April 2016).

Nevertheless, the presence of Chinese enterprises is increasingly felt in global M&A markets. As shown in Figure 1, in 2011, China had 206 overseas acquisitions at US$42.52 billion in total value. In 2015, China had made 382 deals, an increase of 85.4% over 2011. In 2014, deals in mining sector accounted for 32% of the total deals,[24] making it the largest sector in outbound acquisition.

China's state-owned enterprises are mostly concentrated in the energy sector, while privately owned enterprises are in the industrial technology and consumer goods sectors. As see from Table 3, in response to the "One Belt, One Road" initiative, the most active target markets for Chinese buyers are Asia, Europe and North America (Canada and the United States).

The basic purpose of Chinese enterprises' acquisitions of overseas companies is to acquire resources. Apart from the financial support from state-owned banks, such as provision of low interest loans, China has also stationed teams in other countries in search of resources. As the

---

[24] John Zhu, Li Jing and Qu Hongbin, *On the New Silk Road IV: Why China's Overseas Investment Will Keep Growing*, Hong Kong, HSBC, 2016.

Table 3. Outbound M&A Deal Volume by Region of Destination, 2015 vs. 2014

Regions	2014	2015
Africa	7	9
Asia	64	107
Europe	82	110
North America	95	113
South America	6	7
Russia	1	6
Oceania	17	29

Source: David Brown, *PwC M&A 2015 Review and 2016 Outlook*, at <http://www.pwccn.com> (accessed 5 April 2016).

Chinese government provides less direct financial assistance to private enterprises, it would be impossible for private enterprises to carry out large-scale acquisitions of foreign companies without government assistance.

Overseas acquisitions, however, do not guarantee enhanced competitiveness of a firm. Post-acquisition management strategies that are incapable of assimilating the newly acquired overseas companies with the original company's production value chain, brand and market distribution channels may not increase a company's competitiveness. Acquisitions are a shortcut to gaining access to the international markets but they are not a panacea for a company's problems. For an acquisition to be successful, effective post-acquisition teams are needed to deal with capability gaps in areas such as branding and market distribution channels.

Daunting Challenges Ahead

Chinese outward FDI faces a number of formidable challenges. First, the lack of financing support. To provide financial support to Chinese companies expanding abroad, the Export-Import Bank of China was incepted in 1994. However, SOEs are favoured over privately owned companies.

Second, weak domestic capital markets. Very few financial institutions are capable of providing aid to Chinese enterprises in these markets. Their financial assistance is restricted especially to small and medium enterprises and privately owned enterprises.

Third, the lack of accurate information about overseas markets, such as the state of health of the economy of the targeted country, the targeted country's law and regulations pertaining to FDI, market development, business practices and the targeted country's economic relations with China, which is essential for risks and investment suitability assessment.

Fourth, the lack of human capital with international experience and crucial expertise, such as familiarity with the international markets and an understanding of international practices, multinational production, operations and management, etc.

Fifth, the systemic drawbacks of unclear ownership. Most of China's large corporations are state owned or state-owned holding companies and the ambiguity of ownership that is inherent in their governance structure has impeded their efficiency and international competitiveness.

Sixth, a disparity in standards. There is a distinct gap between international practices and Chinese companies' financial management, technology standards, product quality and volume standards, resulting in inefficiencies and impeding Chinese firms' global competitiveness.

Despite the aforementioned challenges, rising overseas investment has helped Chinese enterprises to compete more effectively at the international level and to participate in economic globalisation. Moreover, overseas investment enables Chinese firms to acquire advanced technology and managerial expertise, thereby promoting overall competitiveness.

Chapter 4

Cross-Strait Economic Relations: Taiwan's Perspective

CHIANG Min-Hua*

Over the last few decades, Taiwan-China economic relations have experienced several changes due to the evolving international economic environment as well as political relations. In spite of China's encouragement of Taiwan's investment, cross-strait commercial exchanges were still very restricted by the Kuomintang (KMT) government in Taiwan until the first half of the 1980s. At a time when direct bilateral contact was highly regulated, most of Taiwan's goods, people and financial capital to China were routed through Hong Kong. From the mid-1980s, Taiwan's trade with and travellers to China have been progressively deregulated. Since the early 1990s, Taiwan's gradual relaxation of investment in China further intensified cross-strait economic ties. The close connection in trade and investment between Taiwan and China has paved the way for institutionalised economic relations. When KMT regained power in 2008, greater economic engagement with China was considered a top priority. Between 2008 and 2014, Taiwan and China had reached a variety of agreements ranging from economic cooperation to food safety, tourism, intellectual

---

* CHIANG Min-Hua is Research Fellow at the East Asian Institute, National University of Singapore.

property and so on at the Chiang-Chen Summit. The most noticeable is the signing of the Economic Cooperation Framework Agreement (ECFA) on 29 June 2010 in Chongqing, China. However, the smooth development of institutionalised cross-strait economic relations since 2008 suffered a setback following the Sunflower student movement in March 2014 in Taipei. After Tsai Ing-Wen took office in 2016, cross-strait relations have reached a new low point. China refuses to talk with the Democratic Progressive Party (DPP) government (which is pro-Taiwan independence) unless the latter admits the "92 consensus". Unlike Ma's administration's reliance on China for Taiwan's economic growth, the Tsai administration has sought to look for an economic breakthrough by strengthening Taiwan's relations with developing countries in Southeast Asia and South Asia as well as developed countries in Europe and the United States.

This chapter purports to provide an analytical overview of cross-strait economic relations in the most two recent decades. Through the investigation of bilateral economic relations, it seeks to identify the major challenges and difficulties for deepening Taiwan-China economic relations in the future. The chapter will discuss five issues, namely, Taiwan's investment in China, bilateral trade development, Chinese investment in Taiwan, institutionalised economic engagement, and Taiwan and China's respective roles in East Asia's economic regionalism. The main points and arguments raised would be summarised in the conclusion.

Taiwan's Changing Investments in China

Taiwanese entrepreneurs' investments in China began as early as in the early 1980s. China's economic opening up came at an opportune time when Taiwan's investment environment was worsening (eg. appreciation of New Taiwan dollar following US pressure against Taiwanese exports, higher wages and escalating land cost at home). Beyond the low labour cost, the geographic proximity, similar cultural background and mainland Chinese government's foreign direct investment (FDI) promotion polices have all made China an attractive investment destination for Taiwanese manufacturers. Taiwan government's gradual deregulations since the early 1990s have also propelled Taiwan's investment in China. Beyond the significant investment amounts, since the mid-1990s, there has been a dramatic change of Taiwanese investment from small and medium-sized enterprises (SMEs) to large enterprises and from labour-intensive industries (such as textile, food and plastics and rubber) to information and communications technology (ICT) sectors.

Taiwan's investment in China recorded a new high of US$4.3 billion in 1997 (Figure 1). After the slowdown in 1998 and 1999 due to the Asian financial crisis, Taiwan's investment in China had resurged since 2000. China's entry into the World Trade Organisation (WTO) in 2001 and further economic opening up have greatly promoted Taiwanese investment. Despite the cold political relations across the strait between 2000 and 2008 when Chen Shui-bian was in office, Taiwan's investment in China continued to rise from US$2.6 billion in 2000 to US$9.8 billion in 2008. China's share in Taiwan's total outward investment also doubled from 34% to 69% during the same period. After Ma Ying-jeou took office in 2008, the cordial relations

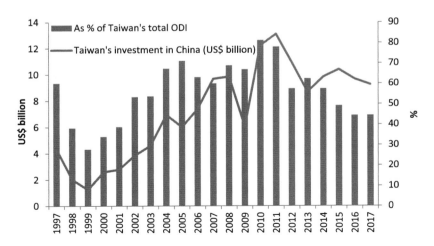

Figure 1.   Taiwan's Investment in China 1997–2017

Source: Investment Commission, Taiwan.

between KMT and the Chinese Communist Party (CCP) had further facilitated business exchanges across the strait. This can be seen from Taiwan's greater investment in China during the first term of Ma's presidency (2008–2012) except during the global financial crisis in 2009. However, after a historical peak of US$13 billion investments in China in 2011, Taiwan's investment in China has started to decline since 2012. In October 2013, the Ma administration relaxed more restrictions on Taiwan's investment in China in several manufacturing and agricultural sectors and basic infrastructures. The most noticeable is the investment deregulation of the petrochemical industry to fill the supply shortage in Taiwan. Semiconductor industries are also allowed to invest in China provided the production technologies in China are at least one generation behind Taiwan's.[1] Even with the further relaxation of rules, Taiwan's investment in China did not grow as much as it did before. Annual investment was around US$9 billion to US$10 billion between 2012 and 2016 when Ma was in office. China's share in Taiwan's total outward investment also registered marked decrease to 44% in 2016 and 2017, from 81% in 2010, notwithstanding the fact that it remains as Taiwan's largest outward invested country.

China's implementation of minimum wage and policy reorientation towards a more consumption-based economy are main reasons behind Taiwan's decreasing investment in China. The investment in China was largely for its low labour cost; Taiwan's manufacturing sectors were the hardest hit by China's wage hike. As shown in Figure 2, manufacturing sectors accounted for 80% to 90% of Taiwan's total investment in China between 1997 and 2009. The share decreased to 56% in 2013 before edging up to 69% in 2017. In comparison, the share of services sectors increased from eight per cent in 2005 to 30% in 2017. Among different service sectors, Taiwan's investment in financial services has progressed most significantly. This could be a result of the progressive deregulation of the outward investment in financial sectors in China. The "Cross-Strait Financial Cooperation Agreement" and memorandums of understanding

---

[1] "Taiwan Lifts Curbs on Petrochemical, Semiconductor Investments in China", *The Wall Street Journal*, 1 October 2013, <http://online.wsj.com/article/DN-CO-20131001-015839.html> (accessed 31 October 2013).

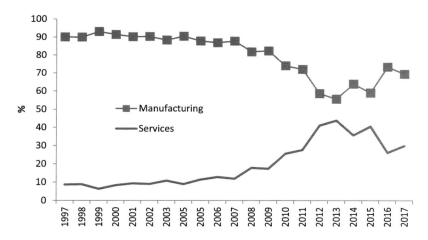

Figure 2. Taiwan's Investment in China by Sector 1997–2017
Source: Investment Commission, Taiwan.

(MOUs) in banking, insurance and securities and futures industries signed in 2009 have provided preferential measures for both sides to enter each other's market. According to the early harvest programme of ECFA, China agreed to open up, with conditions, its banking, insurance, securities and futures sectors for Taiwanese investment whereas Taiwan agreed to open only the banking sectors to China.

China's economic structural changes have also altered Taiwan's investment locations. Unlike 20 years ago when most of Taiwanese investment centred in Fujian and Guangdong provinces, Taiwan investments have shifted to Shanghai and Jiangsu provinces in recent years. In 2015, Shanghai and Jiangsu province accounted for over one third of Taiwan's total investment in China, followed by Beijing (13%) and Guangdong province (13%).[2] Instead of taking advantage of China's cheap labour force, Taiwanese investment in China today tends to tap the potential growth opportunities of the service sectors in the more affluent areas. The higher per capita GDP and growth potential in big cities make them especially attractive for Taiwanese financial institutions to set up branch offices. In particular, Shanghai's potential to become a regional financial

---

[2] Data source: CEIC.

centre in East Asia makes it the top choice for Taiwanese financial firms to put down roots.

Bilateral Trade Development

The immediate consequence of Taiwan's large investment in China is the formation of a division of labour in manufacturing production. Mainland-based Taiwanese companies import intermediate and capital goods from Taiwan to China and export finished goods to developed countries from their manufacturing plants in China. This kind of production network has become especially pronounced after the 2000s when restrictions on direct trade across the strait have been gradually relaxed. In 2001, "three mini links", namely, free sea transportation, merchandise trade and personnel exchanges between Taiwan's two offshore islands — Kinmen and Matsu — and two cities in Fujian province of China (Xiamen and Fuzhou) was initiated. Since 2008, the three links in direct postal, trade and transportation across the Strait have been fully implemented.

As shown in Figure 3, Taiwan's exports to China have started to surpass its imports from China since 2002. The continuously large

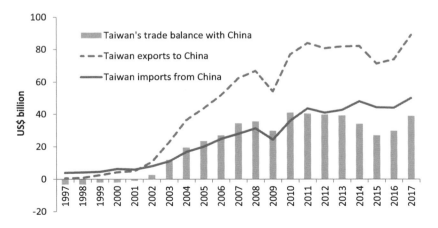

Figure 3. Taiwan's Trade with China 1997–2017
Source: Bureau of Foreign Trade, MOEA, Taiwan.

exports allowed Taiwan to enjoy substantial trade surplus vis-a-vis China in the subsequent years. After hitting a high of US$40 billion of trade surplus with China in 2011, Taiwan's trade surplus had gradually slowed down to US$27 billion in 2015. Due to the slower global demand, Taiwan's deceleration of exporting intermediate goods to China increased. In the meantime, Taiwan's imports of industrial goods from China have steadily increased. Taiwan's trade surplus vis-a-vis China resurged to US$39 billion in 2017. The roll-out of Apple's new devices bolstered the shipment of Taiwan's exports in ICT components.

While Taiwan continued to supply key components to China for final assembly, China has converted from a main producer of labour-intensive products to an important industrial goods source for Taiwanese manufacturers. Unlike 20 years ago when Taiwan imported mostly raw materials (such as iron and coal) and final manufactured products (such as radios, electronic devices and footwear) from China, Taiwan today imports both ICT components (such as electronic integrated circuits) and final ICT products (such as smartphones and computers) from China. Correspondingly, Taiwan's exports to China also changed from intermediate goods for manufacturing textile and chemical industry to key components in ICT sectors. In 2017, Taiwan exported mostly electrical machinery and optical instruments to China (57% of its total exports) and imported mainly electrical machinery from China (44% of its total imports).[3]

Taiwan's export-led economic growth has encountered difficulties in recent years. Its exports to China were stagnant during the 2011–2014 period and declined in 2015 and 2016 (Figure 3). The decreasing investment in manufacturing sectors could have reduced mainland-based Taiwanese companies' demand for industrial goods from Taiwan. While China has quickly developed its manufacturing strength, Taiwan's slow progress in industrial upgrading has narrowed its technology lead over China in recent years. The receding frontier of its technology superiority vis-à-vis China implies Taiwan's

---

[3] Data source: World Trade Atlas.

gradual loss of comparative advantages in exporting high technology and high capital-intensive products to its largest export market. Owing to China's industrial upgrading, there is less demand for the import of intermediate goods from Taiwan. This can be seen from mainland-based Taiwanese firms' change of procurement preference from Taiwan to China. According to a survey done by Taiwan's Ministry of Economic Affairs (MOEA), in 2002, only 19% of Taiwanese firms in China procured capital equipment in China but this percentage increased in 2016 to 81%. During the same period, mainland-based Taiwanese firms' procurement from Taiwan decreased from 54% to 10%.[4]

Several factors account for Taiwan's slow industrial upgrading. First Taiwan's long-term reliance on original equipment manufacturing (OEM), which emphasises on cost saving, instead of innovation, is an important reason behind its incapability to upgrade its industry rapidly. Second, Taiwan's small economic size means that it could devote limited financial resource to R&D. Although Taiwan's R&D expenditure increased from US$15.3 billion in 2005 to US$39.7 billion in 2013, it was only nine per cent of China's in 2013 according to statistics from Taiwan's Ministry of Science and Technology.[5] Third, while there has been a growing return of overseas Taiwanese financial capital in recent years, there are no appropriate measures or good business environment to induce "idle capital" flow to industries. Instead, quite a significant amount of "idle capital" went to the housing and stock markets for the short-term profits. According to Taiwan's official estimates in 2013, there is at least NT$10,000 billion (about US$338 billion) of "idle capital" in the financial market. How to convert "idle capital", mostly from rich entrepreneurs, from speculative investment to "real investment" in industrial development is imperative for advancing Taiwan's industries.

---

[4] *The Investigation and Analysis on the Operation of Investing Business Overseas*, Ministry of Economic Affairs, Taiwan, 2003 and 2017.
[5] Taiwan Ministry of Science and Technology, 2015, <https://ap0512.most.gov.tw/WAS2/technology/AsTechnologyDataIndex.aspx> (accessed 20 March 2016).

Steady Inflow of China's Investment in Taiwan

Since 2009 Taiwan has lifted the ban on inward investment from China. More sectors were opened for mainland Chinese investors in the following years. According to investment rules enacted since 2012, mainland Chinese have been allowed to invest in 204 manufacturing sectors (97% of the total), 161 service sectors (51%) and 43 sectors in public construction (51%) in Taiwan. With the implementation of the early harvest programme under ECFA on 1 January 2011, an additional nine sectors in financial services and business services have been opened to China.

Between 2009 and 2018 (August), China's investment in Taiwan amounted to US$2.1 billion, accounting for three per cent of total inward FDI to Taiwan. China invested mostly in wholesale and retail trade (27% of China's total investment), electronic, computer and optical instruments (13%), machinery and electrical machinery (10%), banking (17%) and harbour (7%) in Taiwan (Figure 4). However, the true investment made by Chinese companies is probably larger. Official data showed that investment from British Overseas Territories in the Caribbean has been the largest source of FDI to Taiwan in recent years.

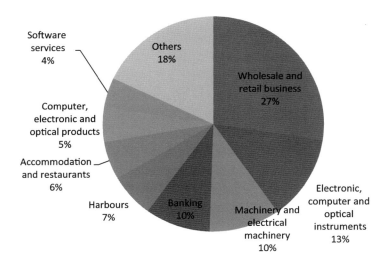

Figure 4. Accumulated China's Investment in Taiwan by Sector 2009-August 2018
Source: Investment Commission, Taiwan.

Between 2009 and 2018 (August), 21% of Taiwan's inward FDI came from this region, probably from Taiwanese companies' "round tripping" to take advantage of incentives aimed at attracting FDI to Taiwan and from Chinese investors who might wish to disguise their origin. In fact, Chinese official data showed a large share of outward investment going to such destinations. Mainland Chinese firms also appear to be investing via subsidiaries in the Netherlands, Hong Kong and Singapore. For instance, Lenova invested in Taiwan through IBM in the Netherlands in 2005. Alibaba had also invested in Taiwan since 2008 through a Singapore-registered company.[6]

Even though there could be mainland Chinese investment from other sources, the total amount was still relatively insignificant compared to Taiwanese investment in China. In 2015 for example, total inward investment to Taiwan was US$5 billion, around half of Taiwan's investment in China (US$10.9 billion). Some Chinese companies' high interest in investing in Taiwan could be motivated by the need to acquire high technology, talents in innovation and management skills. Nevertheless, like other foreign investors, mainland Chinese investors may find the domestic market too small and wages too high as compared to those of other developing countries. Moreover, the overall business environment is not considered very friendly for foreign entrepreneurs. The Taiwan White Paper 2013 released by the American Chamber of Commerce pointed out that the inefficiency of the government is the major obstacle for foreign entrepreneurs to invest in Taiwan. The high income tax rate (45%) on income above NT$10 million (about US$31,000) also deters foreign professionals from accepting jobs in Taiwan. Even with the improved cross-strait relations during Ma's administration, both foreign and domestic companies still encounter difficulties bringing employees in China to work in Taiwan.[7] In February

---

[6] "Alibaba Puts in New Application to Invest in Taiwan: Regulator", *Today*, 6 June 2015, <http://www.todayonline.com/singapore/alibaba-puts-new-application-invest-taiwan-regulator> (accessed 31 March 2016).

[7] *Taiwan White Paper 2013*, American Chamber in Taipei, p. 6, <http://www.amcham.com.tw/ publications/white-papers/cat_view/158-white-paper/310-2013> (accessed 4 December 2013).

2018, Taiwan enacted the Act for the Recruitment and Employment of Foreign Professional Talent. The act has eased rules on visitor, work and residence visas for foreign professionals, including those for their spouses and children. It also makes provisions for retirement benefits, expanded health insurance coverage and tax concessions.[8]

After ECFA, What is Next?

With the early harvest programme under ECFA, China has to lower tariffs on 539 items and Taiwan has been doing the same for 267 Chinese items since January 2011. The aim was to progressively reduce the tariffs of these items to zero by 2013. In terms of trade in services, China opens up 11 service sectors for Taiwanese investments while Taiwan opens nine sectors. Based on the agreed principles under ECFA, six months after the early harvest programme has taken effect, both sides would have to launch negotiations on Cross-Strait Trade in Goods Agreement (CSTGA), Cross-Strait Services Trade (CSSTA), investment agreement and dispute resolution mechanism. To facilitate follow-up negotiations, the Cross-Strait Economic Cooperation Committee (ECC), in its first meeting in February 2011, decided to establish six working groups, including those on trade in goods, trade in services, dispute settlement, investment, industrial cooperation and custom cooperation.

Ma's administration took ECFA as a means to promote Taiwan's economic growth and as being comparable to FTA. On one hand, with over 1.3 billion population, China's domestic market is not only huge but also rapidly growing. Ma considered that greater economic engagement with China would provide Taiwan better opportunities to take advantage of this booming market. On the other hand, Taiwan has been excluded from the growing bilateral and multilateral FTAs trend over the last two decades. Ma's administration believed that ECFA

---

[8] "Taiwan's Foreign Professional Talent Act Goes into Effect", *Taiwan News*, 9 February 2018, <https://www.taiwannews.com.tw/en/news/3360612> (accessed 29 September 2018).

would encourage more countries to follow suit and sign FTAs with Taiwan.

While Ma had much expectation of ECFA reviving the island's economy, the effect of ECFA on Taiwan's overall economy has been limited. After the post-crisis economic rebound in 2010 (with 10.7% of economic growth rate), economic growth has remained weak since 2011. In 2015, economic growth rate even plummeted to merely 0.75%, the lowest since the global financial crisis in 2009. Progress for the FTAs with other countries has also been insignificant. Taiwan signed the economic cooperation agreements with New Zealand (Agreement between New Zealand and the Separate Customs Territory of Taiwan, Penghu, Kinmen and Matsu on Economic Cooperation, ANZTEC) on 16 July 2013 and with Singapore (Agreement between Singapore and the Separate Custom Territory of Taiwan, Penghu, Kinmen and Matzu on Economic Partnership, ASTEP) on 7 November 2013. With Taiwan's other FTA partners, including Panama, Guatemala, Nicaragua, Salvador and Honduras, these seven small economies only accounted for a tiny share of Taiwan's external trade.

The limited effect of ECFA in stimulating the stagnant economy has made further trade negotiation across the strait difficult. Without making any significant economic improvement at home, the government's claims to huge potential benefits from further economic opening up to China was not convincing. Instead, political concerns prevailed. The follow-up trade negotiations under ECFA have made little progress after the 24-day long students' occupation of Taiwan's parliament (Sunflower Student Movement) since 18 March 2014 to stall the CSSTA signed between China and Taiwan. Student protesters believed that the pact was negotiated in secret to give China greater political control of the island. The large-scale students' demonstration was an indication of the unpopularity of Ma's "China rapprochement policy". The election of Tsai Ing-wen (who proposed diversifying diplomatic relations, instead of relying on China alone) in 2016 as Taiwan's president was therefore not a surprise.

Tsai's "New Southward Policy" seeks to strengthen ties with countries in Southeast Asia and India. Unlike the "Southward Policy" in the 1990s, this "New Southward Policy" focuses on not only enhancing bilateral economic relations, but also seeking cooperation in other areas such as climate changes, disease prevention and so on. The DPP government also plans to increase civilian exchange through those with spouses from Southeast Asia. China's booming economy more than 20 years ago explains the ineffectiveness of Taiwan's "Southward Policy" during the 1990s when Lee Teng-hui was in office. With rising labour costs and the slowing down of China's economy in recent years, Tsai's "New Southward Policy" may fit in with the current trend of relocating factories from China to other developing countries in Southeast Asia and India. Besides strengthening relations with countries in the South, the Tsai administration plans to attract Silicon Valley entrepreneurs to invest in Taiwan's manufacturing sector, and enhance Taiwan's innovation capability and supply chain linkage with the United States. Diaspora ties have been sought in this respect. Taiwanese Americans and Taiwanese expatriates are prominent in the US technology sector (among them Jerry Yang, co-founder of Yahoo and Steve Chen, co-founder of YouTube).

Moreover, many Taiwanese firms are alarmed by the escalating US-China trade war in 2018. Many of them have planned to move factories back to Taiwan or to other developing countries. The relocation of manufacturing production from China to other places is particularly noticeable for Taiwanese firms in producing bicycles, communication equipment and servers. Some of them are seeing investments in the United States as new opportunities and responding to President Trump's "America-first manufacturing plan".[9] As early as in August 2017, Hon Hai Precision Industry Co, known as Foxconn Technology Group in China, announced its plan to build a

---

[9] Reviving America's manufacturing industry was a centrepiece during Donald Trump's election campaign. By encouraging US and foreign manufacturers to relocate factories to the United States, Trump expected to create more job opportunities for domestic workers and reduce America's reliance on foreign imports.

US$10 billion factory in Wisconsin, United States, hiring about 13,000 people to make display panel. A few months thereafter in November, another of Hong Hai's investment (worth US$50 million) in US artificial intelligence was approved by Taiwan's investment commission. With China gradually losing its competitiveness in exports, the cross-strait division of labour in manufacturing production will be waning. Some Taiwanese firms may continue to invest in China in order to meet local consumption demand. A new production alliance between Taiwanese manufacturers, Chinese producers and other overseas partners are in the formation. China will no longer be the "global factory". The global factory could be dispersed to many locations. Taiwan will need more diversified FTA network in order to meet future development.

Taiwan and China in East Asian Economic Regionalism

The intensifying cross-strait economic integration has been a spotlight in East Asia's economic dynamism. The quick development of economic regionalism in recent years has also made the institutionalisation of Taiwan-China economic relations a necessity. Apart from the smooth development of cross-strait official talks on economic issues from 2008 to 2014, Taiwan continues to seek FTAs negotiations with other economies. From the government's point of view, it is always too risky putting all the eggs in one basket. Diversifying Taiwan's external economic relations beyond China is one of the principal motivations behind Taiwan's eagerness to negotiate bilateral and multilateral FTAs. The government believed that Taiwan's economy will suffer if excluded from the rapid development of economic regionalism. In particular, Taiwan's main competitor South Korea has been ahead in terms of the number of FTAs signed. While Ma Ying-jeou's administration considered greater economic integration with China as essential to expanding its economic engagement with other countries, Tsai Ing-wen government has turned to develop Taiwan's economic diplomacy with countries in addition to China.

Unlike Taiwan's limited FTA network, China has been quick in developing free trade ties with other economies following its accession to the WTO in 2001. The most significant was its FTA with ASEAN countries, namely, ASEAN+1 in 2002. In 2004, the Agreement on Trade in Goods of the China-ASEAN FTA was signed and entered into force in July 2005. In January 2007, the two parties signed the Agreement on Trade in Services, which took effect in July of the same year. In August 2009, China and ASEAN also signed the Agreement on Investment. Under this Agreement, the six original ASEAN members (Brunei, Indonesia, Malaysia, the Philippines, Singapore and Thailand) and China eliminated tariffs on 90% of their products by 2010. The remaining four countries (Cambodia, Lao PDR, Myanmar and Vietnam) followed suit by 2015. China also concluded separate FTAs with Singapore and New Zealand in 2008. China-South Korea FTA was concluded in 2015. A trilateral FTA between China, South Korea and Japan is underway. At the multilateral level, China is engaging in negotiations with Regional Comprehensive Economic Partnership (RCEP) countries.

Both Taiwan and China will continue to actively engage in institutionalised economic integration at the regional and global levels. Given its influential economic size, China will play a particularly important role in directing the development of economic regionalism. In November 2014, Asia-Pacific economies' agreement to work towards a Chinese-backed Free Trade Area of the Asia-Pacific (FTAAP) during the Asia-Pacific Economic Cooperation (APEC) summit is widely considered as giving Beijing a bigger role in managing regional economic integration. More significantly in April 2015, 57 countries, including several US traditional allies, were approved as founding members of the China-led Asia Infrastructure Investment Bank (AIIB). As China becomes more and more assertive in regional affairs, other countries might have realised that signing an FTA with China is more economically advantageous than signing an FTA with Taiwan. Under the PRC's "one China" policy, it would not be easy for the island to expand its bilateral trade relationship with other nations. The American attitude is therefore important if Taiwan wishes to institutionalise economic relations with countries other than China. Since its initiation in 1994, the Trade and Investment Framework Agreement (TIFA) had been a means for Taiwan to consult the United States on a broad range of economic issues without reaching any significant agreement. Although the current Trump administration supported Taiwan politically, challenges to establishing any economic agreement with the United States remain. First, to gain US support, Taiwan will have to open its market to American agricultural products. Second, interests groups may try to deter Taiwan's trade liberalisation to protect the interests of domestic firms and workers. It may also take a longer time for the Taiwanese government to come up with remedial measures.

Conclusion

China's "opening up policy" to attract FDI since the end of the 1970s has not only helped the country to modernise itself, but also strengthened its economic ties with Taiwan. The development of cross-strait economic relations over the past three decades can be summarised as follows. First, despite the Taiwanese government's strict outward investment policy towards China, many Taiwanese businessmen continued to invest in China through Hong Kong or their holding companies registered in the British Overseas Territories in the Caribbean since the 1980s. Nonetheless, China's wage hike since more than a decade ago has altered this cost-driven investment. Service investment aimed at tapping the booming Chinese market is becoming more vital.

Second, the investments promoted bilateral trade, in particular Taiwan's exports of intermediate goods to China for final assembly. Following China's wage hike and industrial upgrading, the bilateral trade direction has changed. Taiwan today imports not only final goods but also industrial goods from China. China's growing share in Taiwan's imports implies that the country plays an increasingly important role in Taiwan's domestic manufacturing production.

Third, Chinese investment in Taiwan has been growing since its deregulation in 2009. As Taiwan's market is small, Chinese investors tend to focus on transferring technology and skills from Taiwan to develop a larger market in China. As the Tsai Ing-wen administration is cautious about further economic opening up to China, Chinese investment in Taiwan in the coming years could be under more stringent examination. This may discourage investment from China.

Fourth, while Ma's administration expected the ECFA to revive the island's economy, the result from the deeper institutionalised economic integration with China was frustrating. Without generating noticeable economic progress, deeper institutionalised integration with China would only raise the concern that the island could eventually lose its political sovereignty. Although greater economic engagement with China or other economies is a necessity in a globalised world, it is not a guarantee that Taiwan's comparative advantages *vis-à-vis* its competitors in the region would be improved. The most pressing work for Taiwan at present is to upgrade its domestic industries through innovation and integration, and to find an indispensable position in the region to avoid being marginalised during the wave of regional economic integration.

Finally China has not only signed several bilateral FTAs with other countries but also looking at becoming an important player in multilateral trade negotiations. Unlike China's active participation in various forms of economic cooperation and agreements, Taiwan's isolation in the international community has obstructed its progress in securing more FTAs. However, China's growing influence in economic regionalism has raised concerns about potential competition with the United States in the Asia-Pacific region. Taiwan may have greater opportunities of joining multinational FTAs during the course of growing China-US conflict on a variety of economic and political issues. Taiwan will have to make tremendous effort in adjusting its domestic regulations to meet global standards and requirements. On the other hand, given the geographical proximity and China's huge market, China could still remain as an important outward investment destination and trading partner for Taiwan. The finalising of free trade in goods and services agreements with China remains important. Taiwan's quest to expand economic diplomacy with other developing countries in the future is highly contingent on how the Tsai administration handles its China relations.

Chapter 5

CEPA and Mainland-Hong Kong's Economic Relations

ZHANG Yang*

Hong Kong's economy has experienced ebb and flow since 1997. It was hit by the catastrophic ripples of the Asian financial crisis in 1998, the global economic downturn in 2001 and the outbreak of SARS (severe acute respiratory syndrome) in 2003. To revive the post-SARS economy and kick-start the recovery, Mainland-Hong Kong Closer Economic Partnership Arrangement" (CEPA), the first free trade agreement between the two sides, was concluded in June 2003, tailored to the strengths and development potential of both parties. Through the CEPA Main Text and the 10 supplements signed annually subsequently, together with the most recent investment agreement signed on 28 June 2017, wide-ranging liberalisation measures have opened up new business opportunities for Hong Kong and mainland enterprises. Since the implementation of CEPA, there had been a strong rebound in consumption, an end to prolonged deflation, a revival in private investment and a hefty economic growth performance. GDP (gross domestic product) reverted from a negative 0.7% decline in 2003 to a growth rate exceeding six

---

* ZHANG Yang is Associate Professor of Business Economics at the Faculty of Business Administration, University of Macau.

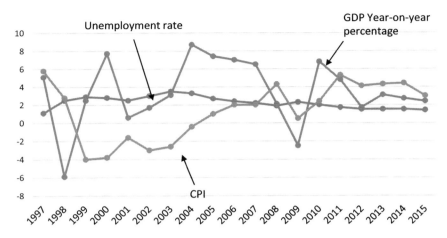

Figure 1. Hong Kong's Macro Economy Indicators: 1997–2015
Source: Hong Kong Census and Statistics Department.

per cent on the back of mainland China's double-digit growth until the global financial crisis (Figure 1). Although the range of impressive statistics may not be fully attributable to CEPA, the trade accord has certainly been conducive to liberalising trade and investment as well as boosting market sentiment, thus facilitating the economic renewal of Hong Kong. In the post-crisis years, the expansion has more than halved with an average growth rate of 3.6 from 2010 to 2015.

CEPA and Its Latest Development

Signed in June 2003 and effective on 1 January 2004, CEPA aims to strengthen economic cooperation between the two sides and promote joint development through progressive tariff elimination, trade liberalisation and investment facilitation. Under a building block mechanism, annual supplements to CEPA have been introduced in each subsequent year with the scope of liberalisation further extended in both depth and breadth upon negotiation and consensus between Hong Kong and the central authority in Beijing.

Supplement I to CEPA took effect in early 2005 adding 729 types of products with Hong Kong origin to the zero-tariff list covered by

CEPA, allowing a total of 1,108 types of such products with tariff rates ranging from three per cent to 33.3% to enter the Mainland tariff-free. Supplement I also opened up eight new areas for Hong Kong service providers and further relaxed the business scope for some of the 18 service sectors already opened under CEPA.

On 18 October 2005 Supplement II was reached and came into force on 1 January 2006. Tariff-free treatment was further extended to all Hong Kong products that meet CEPA Rules of Origin.[1] Supplement II allows products covered in 1,369 tariff codes to enter the mainland market at zero import tariffs upon obtaining a Certificate of Hong Kong Origin. Fifteen liberalisation measures were also introduced, granting Hong Kong service suppliers preferential access to the mainland market in 27 service areas.

Subsequently through Supplements III to X, the Mainland gradually relaxed market access conditions in more areas. According to Supplement IV, the minimum total asset requirement for a Hong Kong bank acquiring a shareholding in a mainland bank was lowered from US$10 billion to US$6 billion. The required capital investment for setting up equity or contractual joint venture medical and dental institutions was reduced from US$2.6 million to US$1.3 million. In tourism, the minimum annual business turnover of Hong Kong travel agents to set up joint venture and wholly owned travel agents in the Mainland was reduced to US$8 million and US$15 million respectively (down from US$12 million and US$25 million).

Supplement VIII to CEPA, signed on 13 December 2011 and effective on 1 January 2012, allowed traders to include the value of raw materials and component parts originated from the Mainland when calculating the "value-added content". For service trade, market access conditions were further relaxed in 13 existing sectors and three new sectors including inter-disciplinary research and experimental development services; services incidental to manufacturing; and library, museum and other cultural services.

---

[1] Prohibited articles such as waste electrical machinery and surgical products, chemical residual, municipal waste, tiger bone and rhinoceros horn are not included.

The Agreement on Trade in Services signed on 27 November 2015 was for implementation from 1 June 2016. The Agreement makes reference to the framework of the Agreement between the Mainland and Hong Kong on Achieving Basic Liberalisation of Trade in Services in Guangdong (the Guangdong Agreement) signed in December 2014 and extends the geographical coverage from Guangdong to the whole Mainland. Specifically, 28 liberalisation measures were introduced for cross-border trade in services including banking, legal, accounting, telecommunications and cultural services. The Agreement allows foreign firms to use Hong Kong as a springboard to China's vast market. The deal also includes the Most-Favoured Treatment clause, assuring Hong Kong of access to benefits secured from any subsequent liberalisation agreements by China with other economies.

The most recent development under the CEPA framework was the Investment Agreement and Agreement on Economic and Technical Cooperation signed on 28 June 2017, further broadening the scope of CEPA as a comprehensive free trade agreement (FTA) covering investment as well as economic and technical cooperation on top of trade in goods and trade in services.

Implementation of CEPA and Its Impact

CEPA has gradually expanded the categories of tariff-free products and since 1 January 2006, the Mainland has fully implemented zero tariff treatment on all imported goods of Hong Kong origin. As at the end of June 2007, the Hong Kong Trade and Industry Department had granted 24,174 Hong Kong manufacturers the Certificate of Origin (CO),[2] a licence for Hong Kong manufacturers to export their products to China at zero tariff under the framework of CEPA.

---

[2] The eligibility criterion is rules of origin, that is, the goods must be wholly obtained in Hong Kong or have undergone substantial transformation in Hong Kong, regardless of the ownership or the source of capital of the manufacturers.

As of April 2007, Hong Kong exports to China under this arrangement were reported to be over US$1 billion.[3] The immediate benefit that these manufacturers enjoy from the zero-tariff access is clearly the savings on costs. As of June 2007, about US$91 million of tariffs had been waived according to the Chinese customs.[4] In the first quarter of 2007, 10.6% of the domestic exports from Hong Kong to the mainland market enjoyed zero-tariff treatment, up from three per cent in 2004. This accounted for 4.1% of total domestic exports of Hong Kong in the same period.

By mid-2016 the number of CO obtained has substantially soared to 140,163. Table 1 shows that most of the manufacturers that obtained CO are from the food and beverages (27.8%) sector, followed by textiles and clothing sector (19.7%), plastics and plastic articles (21.3%) and pharmaceuticals (11.0%). Companies such as Mei-Xin (Hong Kong), Lee Kum Kee, Eu Yan Sang (Hong Kong), Beijing Tong Ren Tang Chinese Medicine Company, Swire Coca-Cola Hong Kong, among others, make use of the zero-tariff preference.

Hong Kong's manufacturing activities have been gradually shifted to the Mainland for its low cost labour and as a result CEPA would be more effective in enhancing Hong Kong's service sector. As a matter of fact, this sector contributed 92.7% of the territory's GDP in 2014 (Figure 2). Among Hong Kong's major service sectors, tradeable services such as wholesale, retail, restaurants and hotels, finance, insurance, real estate, business, and social and personal services account for more than 20% of Hong Kong's GDP. With the objective of intensifying the service links between Hong Kong and China, CEPA enables Hong Kong to better utilise its comparative advantage in the service sector vis-à-vis the Mainland, allowing Hong Kong service providers to be the biggest beneficiary of this arrangement.

---

[3] "Impact of the First Three Phases of CEPA on the Hong Kong Economy", available at <http://www.legco.gov.Hong Kong/yr06-07/english/panels/ci/papers/ci0612cb1-1849-4-e.pdf> (accessed 21 July 2016).

[4] "An Agreement in Numbers", People's Daily Online, 29 June 2007, available at <http://english.peopledaily.com.cn/200706/29/eng20070629_388719.html> (accessed 21 July 2016).

Table 1. Breakdown of Certificate of Hong Kong Origin Statistics by Product Types (as at 30 June 2016)

	Product Types	Cumulative No. of CO Applications Received	Cumulative No. of COs Approved
1	Food and Beverages	40,086	38,973
2	Food Residues and Animal Fodder	289	286
3	Mineral Products	1	—
4	Chemical Products	8,325	8,152
5	Pharmaceutical Products	15,723	15,502
6	Colouring Matters	3,567	3,514
7	Cosmetics	309	286
8	Plastics and Plastic Articles	30,262	29,907
9	Leather and Furskin Articles	1,490	1,459
10	Paper and Printed Articles	3,919	3,831
11	Textiles and Clothing	28,363	27,615
12	Glass and Glassware	2	—
13	Jewellery and Precious Metals	742	735
14	Base Metal Products	5,997	5,959
15	Machinery and Mechanical Appliances	771	748
16	Electrical and Electronic Products	2,074	2,011
17	Optical, Photographic and Cinematographic Instruments and Parts	840	773
18	Medical Instruments and Massage Apparatus	18	17
19	Measuring and Checking Instruments and Parts	133	133
20	Clocks and Watches and Parts Thereof	1,038	1,012
21	Furniture	36	34
22	Toys and Games or Sports Requisites	1	1
23	Miscellaneous	5	5
	Total (Note)	143,171	140,162

Note: The total figure may not be equal to the sum of all Product Types as one CO (CEPA) can cover products of more than one type.
Source: Hong Kong Trade Development Council.

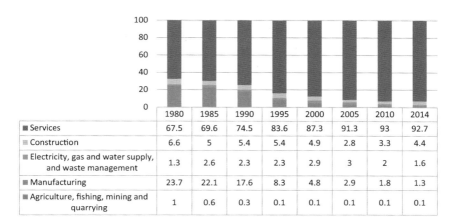

Figure 2. Composition of Hong Kong's GDP by Sector (%)
Source: Hong Kong Census and Statistics Department.

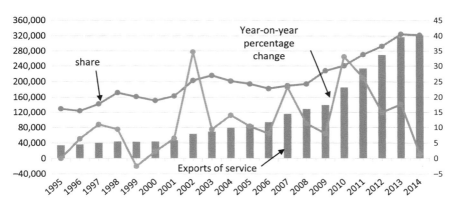

Figure 3. Hong Kong's Export of Services to Mainland China, 1995–2014 (Million HK$ and %)
Source: Hong Kong Census and Statistics Department.

The market liberalisation and facilitation measures under CEPA mostly cover pillar industries in which Hong Kong has a competitive edge, consolidating Hong Kong's status as an international financial, trade, shipping and logistics centre. More importantly, by relaxing stringent capital, asset, turnover and other operational requirements, CEPA has lowered the thresholds of entry for Hong Kong companies to the Mainland's service industry. Reducing the costs for companies seeking market entry would facilitate mid-size Hong Kong companies to enter China, which may otherwise be marginalised. As of 30 September 2018, over 3,239 Hong Kong-registered enterprises in sectors ranging from banking to logistics had been issued Certificates of Hong Kong Service Supplier (Table 2). Among them, 45.5% were from the transport and logistics services sector and 11.9% from distribution services.

In the banking sector, CEPA has effectively allowed almost all of the eight medium-sized Hong Kong banks to enter the mainland market thanks to the easing of restrictions for operation in the Mainland. By 2004, 58 Hong Kong-based banks including 45 branches, 10 sub-branches, one financial company and two joint venture banks[5] had opened branches in the Mainland. Thirty-eight banks are allowed to conduct Chinese currency business for individuals, covering deposits, remittances and currency exchanges and six Hong Kong banks were allowed to do online business in the Mainland.[6]

Under CEPA, Hong Kong professionals in the securities and insurance industries can apply to practise in the Mainland; legal and medical practitioners from Hong Kong are allowed to sit for the Mainland's qualification examination. Hong Kong residents are allowed to practise in mainland law firms provided they are not simultaneously employed by the representative office of a foreign law firm. Hong Kong's lawyers and barristers can become involved in civil litigation cases on the Mainland while Hong Kong-qualified legal practitioners can act as mainland lawyers in matrimonial and succession cases relating to Hong Kong.[7]

---

[5] "The 4th Consultation of the CBRC and the HKMA Was Held in Hong Kong", China Banking Regulatory Commission, 13 July 2005, available at <http://www.cbrc.gov.cn/chinese/home/docView/1480.html> (accessed 21 July 2016).

[6] "58 Hong Kong Banks Have Branches in China's Inland Cities", People's Daily Online, 31 December 2004, available at <http://english.people.com.cn/200412/31/eng20041231_169268.html> (accessed 21 July 2016).

[7] Jonathan Yeung, "CEPA 'a Boon' Both for Hong Kong and Mainland", *China Daily – Hong Kong Edition*, 27 July 2006, available at <http://www.lifeofguangzhou.com/node_10/node_37/node_84/2006/07/27/11539652556013.shtml> (accessed 21 July 2016).

Table 2. Certificate of Hong Kong Service Supplier (As of 30 September 2018)

	Service Sector	Cumulative Number of Certificates of Hong Kong Service Supplier Issued
1	Legal services	24
2	Accounting, auditing and bookkeeping services	3
3	Construction professional services and construction and related engineering services	104
4	Medical and dental services	47
5	Computer and related services and information technology services	23
6	Real estate services	29
7	Advertising services	142
8	Market research services	0
9	Management consulting and related services	52
10	Mining and prospecting services	0
11	Research and experimental development services on natural sciences and engineering	2
12	Public utility services	1
13	Placement and supply services of personnel	168
14	Building-cleaning services	1
15	Photographic services	3
16	Printing services	121
17	Translation and interpretation services	0
18	Convention and exhibition services	24
19	Value-added telecommunications services	64
20	Telecommunication services	4
21	Audiovisual services	84
22	Distribution services	364
23	Environmental services	2
24	All insurance and insurance-related services	23
25	Banking and other financial services (excluding insurance and securities)	10
26	Securities and futures services	91

(*Continued*)

Table 2. (*Continued*)

	Service Sector	Cumulative Number of Certificates of Hong Kong Service Supplier Issued
27	Social services	0
28	Tourism and travel related services	51
29	Cultural services (excluding audiovisual services)	36
30	Sporting services	0
31	Transport and logistics services	1,402
32	Air transport services	300
33	Trademark agency services	15
34	Specialty design services	0
35	Interdisciplinary research and experimental development services	0
36	Services incidental to manufacturing	8
37	Library, museum and other cultural services	0
38	Services related to agriculture, forestry and fishing	1
39	Administrative and support services	16
40	Education services	6
41	Personal, pet and household services	0
42	Other business services	6
43	Other professional services	0
44	Other research and development services	0
45	Rental/leasing services	4
46	Communication services	0
47	Other human health services	5
48	After-death services facilities	0
49	Duplicating services	0
50	Factoring services	3
51	Publication-related services	0
52	Technical testing and analysis services	1
53	Security and guarding services	0
	Total	3,239

Source: Hong Kong Trade Development Council.

In addition, Hong Kong permanent residents with Chinese citizenship are permitted to set up retail stores in all provinces and municipalities. By March 2006, 2,040 stores had been set up by Hong Kong residents in the Mainland, among which 89 were in Guangdong.[8] One prominent Hong Kong enterprise was reportedly operating 62 convenience stores in Guangdong province and another health and beauty retailer opened 200 outlets in China by June 2006.

In the first year of its implementation, CEPA reportedly generated about HK$1.6 billion worth of service receipts from companies in the 18 service sectors engaged in the export of services to the Mainland. According to a report by HKTID assessing CEPA's impact from 2004 to 2006, CEPA generated US$1.2 billion worth of services receipts from companies in 22 services sectors, 4.4% of total service receipts. Distribution sectors recorded the largest CEPA-induced export of services, followed by hotels and travel agencies, as well as freight.[9] On employment, CEPA generated 36,000 new jobs for Hong Kong residents, 1,000 positions of which were in the Mainland. New positions created were able to accommodate more than 23% of total unemployed persons in 2006, thus mitigating Hong Kong's unemployment problem for the period. Between 2004 and 2006, CEPA induced about US$652 million additional capital investments in Hong Kong. Among the investments, the manufacturing sector absorbed about US$13 million in 2005 and US$28.5 million in 2006 but a much bigger amount went to the service sectors. By 2006, the cumulative amount of additional capital investment in the service sectors was about US$614 million. The distribution services, freight transport and logistics services contributed to the bulk of additional investment.

During the 2007–2009 period, CEPA-induced business receipts totalled HK$55.1 billion for companies in Hong Kong. In cumulative terms, Hong Kong service providers have enjoyed HK$61.1

---

[8] Jonathan Yeung, "CEPA 'a Boon' Both for Hong Kong and Mainland".
[9] "Impact on the Hong Kong Economy of CEPA", Trade and Industry Department website, available at <http://www.legco.gov.hk/yr06-07/english/panels/ci/papers/ci0612cb1-1849-4-e.pdf> (accessed 21 July 2016).

billion from their mainland-related business due to CEPA and its supplements. Their operations on the Mainland generated an even larger sum of HK$198.5 billion from 2007 to 2009, mainly from freight forwarding agencies, distribution, advertising/audiovisual, and transport and logistics. As at end-2009, due to the liberalisation of trade in services under CEPA, 55,066 jobs were created in Hong Kong and 40,600 jobs in the Mainland.

Overall, the implementation of CEPA and its supplements has fully eliminated tariffs for imported goods of Hong Kong origin upon applications by local manufacturers and upon the CEPA origin rules being agreed and met. In addition, the Mainland has opened up 153 service sectors to Hong Kong, 95.6% of the 160 service sectors under the WTO classification. National treatment will be applied to Hong Kong in 62 sectors. As a stimulus package to foster growth for the Hong Kong's economy, CEPA unleashes opportunities and market access for the territory's businesses and service suppliers in mainland China through the progressive implementation of liberalisation and cooperation measures. The materialisation and expansion of CEPA had helped revive the sagging post-SARS Hong Kong economy which registered a solid average annual growth of 7.3% from 2004 to 2007.

CEPA Lifts Hong Kong-Mainland Economic Interaction to a New Level

Hong Kong has served effectively as a gateway to the Mainland and accordingly intimate economic ties have developed between the two sides. Since 1985 mainland China has been Hong Kong's largest trade partner in imports and re-exports, and the largest destination of domestic exports as well. With the implementation of CEPA, this economic tie has further strengthened. Except for 2009, Hong Kong's merchandise trade relationship with the Mainland has seen steady increase since 2000. The Mainland is getting increasingly important as a partner of Hong Kong's trade in goods, both as a top export destination and a top import supplier, as is shown in Figure 4. In 2015, 49% of imports were

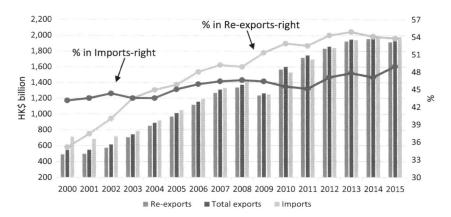

Figure 4. Hong Kong's Merchandise Trade with Mainland (HK$ billion and %)
Source: Hong Kong Census and Statistics Department.

of China origin while 54% of exports were destined for the Mainland. In 2012, Hong Kong overtook Japan as the Mainland's second largest trading partner after the United States, accounting for 8.7% of its total trade in 2015.

Similar trend can also be observed in services trade. Hong Kong's export of service to the Mainland has increased considerably over time and the Mainland has become Hong Kong's single largest destination for the export of its services accounting for 40.3% of total in 2014, up from 22.8% in 2006 (Figure 5). In 2010, exports of service to the Mainland recorded a 33.1% year-on-year growth followed by a 26.2% increase in 2011, 15% in 2012, 17.7% in 2013 before slowing down to a 1.4% rise in 2014.

The enhanced economic interaction between Hong Kong and the Mainland is also reflected by the increase in people-to-people exchanges. The Individual Visit Scheme (IVS) programme under the framework of CEPA was introduced in 2003[10] and has induced incremental arrivals as visitors increase their travelling frequency as a result of the

---

[10] IVS was first implemented on 28 July 2003 and now IVS covers 49 cities in the Mainland with a population exceeding 250 million.

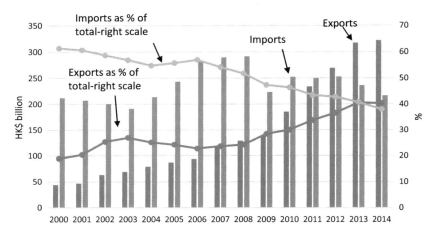

Figure 5. Hong Kong's Trade in Service with Mainland (HK$ billion and %)
Source: Hong Kong Census and Statistics Department.

convenience and flexibility brought about by the scheme. As of the end of 2006, mainland residents made 17.2 million trips to Hong Kong under the IVS, 39% of all the trips by mainland visitors during the same period.[11] Additional tourist spending generated by IVS visitors was estimated to be about US$2.9 billion between 2004 and 2006, with major spending made in retail, hotel and restaurants. In cumulative terms, during the 2004–09 period, IVS visitors brought about additional spending totalling over HK$84.8 billion.[12] By March 2010, over 49 million mainland visitors had visited Hong Kong under the scheme. In 2012, of the almost 35 million mainland visitors to Hong Kong, two thirds came under CEPA's IVS.

Besides the influx of people, CEPA is believed to have facilitated mainland investment to Hong Kong. The inflow of mainland direct investment had amounted to US$448 billion at the end of 2014 or

---

[11] "Impact on the Hong Kong Economy of CEPA", Trade and Industry Department.
[12] "2010 Update of CEPA's Impact on the Hong Kong Economy", Trade and Industry Department website, available at <http://www.legco.gov.hk/yr09-10/english/panels/ci/papers/cicb1-2065-1-e.pdf > (accessed 21 July 2016).

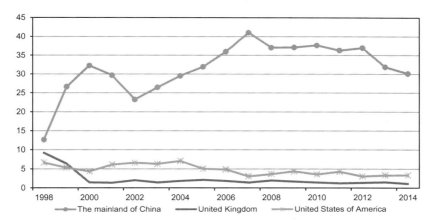

Figure 6. Share of Total Foreign Direct Investment in Hong Kong (%)
Source: Hong Kong Census and Statistics Department.

30% of Hong Kong's total inward investment, up from barely a 10th of the total in the late 1990s, while the roles of the United Kingdom and the United States have become less important as source countries (Figure 6). Some mainland enterprises looking to expand their global horizons have utilised Hong Kong's international connectivity and used it as a key offshore capital-raising centre. In 2012, about 2000 mainland firms were allowed to invest in Hong Kong for over US$46.5 billion. As of December 2015, a total of 951 mainland enterprises were listed in the Hong Kong Stock Exchange (both the Main Board and GEM), accounting for 51% of the total number of listed companies and 62% of total market capitalisation.[13]

Significant breakthrough in deepening financial integration between the Mainland and Hong Kong came in November 2014 when the Shanghai–Hong Kong Stock Connect initiative was launched, allowing investments in each other's stock markets and essentially opening China's closely guarded stock market to any foreigner with a

---

[13] <http://hong-kong-economy-research.hktdc.com/business-news/article/Market-Environment/Economic-and-Trade-Information-on-Hong-Kong/etihk/en/1/1X000000/1X09OVUL.htm> (accessed 21 July 2016).

Hong Kong brokerage account. In July 2015, mutual funds domiciled in Shanghai or Hong Kong were allowed to be sold in each other's markets, giving a boost to Hong Kong's asset management industry. The Shenzhen-Hong Kong Stock Connect was launched within the year of 2016.

By allowing freer cross-border capital and goods flow as well as people and expertise exchanges, CEPA provides Hong Kong's service suppliers with wider access to the 1.3 billion population market and an economic platform for effectively transferring management skills and knowledge to the Mainland, reinforcing Hong Kong's position as a world-class service-oriented economy. Hong Kong's advanced service sector to a greater extent can be considered as a complement to the Mainland's booming economy. CEPA therefore is often perceived as a mechanism for deepening regional economic integration and as a result Hong Kong's economy has become more interwoven with that of the Mainland.

Way Ahead

For the year 2018, Hong Kong's economy was forecast to grow by 3.4% on the back of a moderate loosening of fiscal policy. However, an escalation of trade conflicts between the United States and China has cast a cloud over the outlook for Hong Kong's export sector and trade growth. Following the recent interest rate hike by the Fed, the Hong Kong Monetary Authority is expected to further raise its base rate in 2019 and higher borrowing costs are likely to lead to a property market correction amid tighter local credit conditions, thus curbing property investment and overall growth. With mainland China, Hong Kong's services trade will continue to post large and growing surpluses, supported by inflows of tourists and exports of professional services associated with business in mainland China. With its prime location, access to top talent, pro-business culture, friendly regulatory and tax environments and world-class infrastructure, Hong Kong is well-placed to function as a key link for the China's Belt and Road Initiative (BRI) that opens up immense opportunities to Hong Kong's financial services companies, lawyers, construction firms and transportation companies among others. Hong Kong's economic future will be largely determined by how well it can hold on to its unique position as an international trading city and capitalise on the BRI and other initiatives of the central government.

Chapter 6

China–ASEAN Economic Relations Remain Resilient Despite Rising Challenges

Sarah Y TONG and KONG Tuan Yuen*

Bilateral economic relations between China and the Association of Southeast Asian Nations (ASEAN) have developed rapidly and significantly in recent decades, with the two sides continuing to strengthen economic ties. Since the early 1990s, China has placed great emphasis on developing economic relations with ASEAN. In 1991, both sides launched a dialogue process and, in 1996, China became ASEAN's full dialogue partner. In 2003, ASEAN–China relations were upgraded to the strategic partnership level. Following China's accession to the World Trade Organisation, ASEAN and China signed the Framework Agreement on Comprehensive Economic Cooperation, which started the process of building the China–ASEAN Free Trade Area (CAFTA) in 2002.[1] Further, in 2014, both sides

---

* Sarah Y Tong is Senior Research Fellow at the East Asian Institute, National University of Singapore; Kong Tuan Yuen is Visiting Research Fellow at the same institute.
[1] In January 2010, CAFTA was fully established, cutting tariffs on 7,881 product categories, or 90% of goods exported to China, ASEAN-5 and Brunei, to zero. The remaining four ASEAN countries will follow suit in 2015. See "China–ASEAN FTA Pact Set to Boost Trade Volume", *China Daily*, 30 December 2009, <http://www.chinadaily.com.cn/china/2009-12/30/content_9244077.htm> (accessed 30 May 2015).

launched negotiations on upgrading CAFTA, focusing on key areas of trade in goods, service trade, dispute settlement and investment.[2]

Sustaining Bilateral Economic Linkages

Bilateral trade is central to China–ASEAN economic relations. China has been ASEAN's largest trading partner since 2009, while ASEAN has been China's third-largest importer since 2010. As total bilateral trade expands, China's relative importance as a trading partner of ASEAN rose faster than it would be the vice versa despite the increasingly unbalanced bilateral trade. China's trade with newer ASEAN members grew faster than that with the ASEAN-6 countries of Indonesia, Malaysia, Singapore, Thailand, the Philippines and Brunei. China–ASEAN bilateral investment has also been strengthened in recent years. China's outbound direct investment has risen substantially since the early 2000s, following the government's "going out" initiative. Bilateral economic linkage also took on other forms, including tourism, trade in services, financial cooperation and various joint projects.

China is committed to further improving its relations with its neighbours through collaboration in its initiatives like the 21st-Century Maritime Silk Road, Asian Infrastructure Investment Bank (AIIB) and Silk Road Fund. China and ASEAN are likely to become a strong driving force for regional development and infrastructure construction. China–ASEAN strategic partnership will thus develop into a broader and deeper cooperation. Improvements to regional connectivity and accessibility will boost ASEAN's economy.

However, challenges abound when further strengthening bilateral economic relations. As the world economy remains weak and China's economy undergoes restructuring and experiences a deceleration in growth, it is less certain that closer bilateral cooperation could reap economic benefit. Meanwhile, there is still a lack of trust between China and ASEAN. On the one hand, regional neighbours treated China's sincerity

---

[2] "ASEAN–China Relations", ASEAN–China Centre, April 2015, at <http://www.asean-china-center.org/english/2015-04/13/c_13365143.htm> (accessed 30 May 2015).

with scepticism because of its rapid economic rise and its inability to articulate its intentions clearly in regional affairs. On the other hand, the engagement with outside big powers by some ASEAN members also evokes a certain degree of misgiving in China. In particular, the recent escalation of the South China Sea conflict can derail China–ASEAN bilateral economic relations if it is not managed carefully and skilfully.

Bilateral Trade Essential to China–ASEAN Economic Relations

Trade between China and ASEAN began to grow substantially since the 1980s, along with China's efforts to expand its economic relations with the rest of the world after adopting a grand reform agenda in 1978. Bilateral trade has expanded to a great extent since the early 1990s when China opened up its economy further, following Deng Xiaoping's *Nanxun* (southern tour) in 1992. China's accession to the World Trade Organisation in 2001 marked a new beginning of China's expansion of trade with the world and ASEAN. China has been ASEAN's largest trading partner since 2009 and ASEAN is China's third-largest trading partner since 2010.[3]

Table 1 shows the growth rate of China–ASEAN bilateral trade. Between 1981 and 2014, ASEAN's total trade with China rose by 17% per year on average. China began to report its trade volume with ASEAN since 1997. Between 1997 and 2014, China's total trade with ASEAN grew by 19% per year on average. Annual growth in bilateral trade increased from 15% between 1997 and 2001 to 28% between 2001 and 2008, followed by a deceleration in growth to about 13% per year in recent years. Since 2001, China's exports to ASEAN grew faster than its imports from ASEAN, while the reverse is true from 1997 to 2001. Although there are gaps between values reported by trading partners, the two sets of trade data have shown similar trend over time.

---

[3] "China–ASEAN Trade, Investment Has Room to Deepen", *China Daily*, 9 August 2014, at <http://www.chinadaily.com.cn/world/2014-08/09/content_18278923.htm> (accessed 14 July 2016).

Table 1. China–ASEAN Bilateral Trade Growth

	Exports	Imports	Total
ASEAN's trade with China (annual growth %)			
1981–1991	19.4	11.7	13.9
1991–2001	17.7	13.4	15.2
2001–2008	27.0	28.3	27.7
2008–2014	10.8	13.9	12.6
1981–2014	**18.8**	**16.0**	**16.8**
China's trade with ASEAN (annual growth %)			
1997–2001	11.5	17.4	14.6
2001–2008	29.6	26.0	27.7
2008–2014	15.6	10.1	13.0
1997–2014	**20.1**	**18.2**	**19.2**

Sources: Calculated by the authors from International Monetary Fund, *Direction of Trade of ASEAN Countries*; and CEIC Data Manager.

The highly continuous growth in trade between China and ASEAN will have important implications for ASEAN. China's economic interaction with ASEAN has grown rapidly and significantly, even during the relatively turbulent post-2008 period. Indeed, China and ASEAN countries have become significant economic partners as regional production network in Asia has strengthened and grown both in size and scope. Despite the imbalance in bilateral trade, structural changes in China's economy and trade are expected to narrow the gap by generating more opportunities for ASEAN countries. Understandably, given the different levels of development among ASEAN countries, the impact of China's changing dynamics will also differ considerably. For example, China's efforts to upgrade its industry and trade will benefit the relatively less developed ASEAN members, while this also implies that countries with similar development level as China would face intensifying competition.

While total bilateral trade between China and ASEAN has expanded strongly over the past few decades, their trade relations showed several

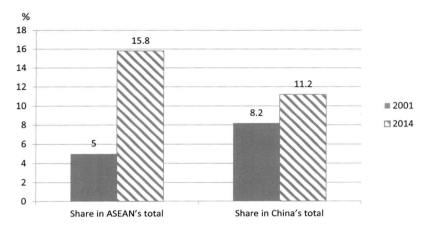

Figure 1. Share of Bilateral Trade in ASEAN's and China's Total Trade, 2001–2014
Source: Calculated by the authors from International Monetary Fund, *Direction of Trade of ASEAN Countries*; and CEIC Data Manager.

different tendencies. First, China's relative importance as a trading partner of ASEAN rose faster than it would be vice versa. In the 2001–2014 period, the share of China–ASEAN bilateral trade in ASEAN's total trade increased by about 10%, from 5% to 15.8%, while the share of bilateral trade in China's total trade only increased by three percentage points, from 8.2% to 11.2% (Figure 1). Before 2000, ASEAN as a trading partner was more important to China as compared to China's relative importance to ASEAN. This has been reversed since then and ASEAN's trade with China now constitutes a larger share in ASEAN's total trade compared to ASEAN's share in China's total trade. According to China's Ministry of Commerce, China–ASEAN trade hit US$472.16 billion in 2015 from US$7.96 billion in 1991, growing at 18.5% annually. In 2015, China had been ASEAN's biggest trading partner, while ASEAN was China's third-largest trading partner.[4]

---

[4] "Boom in China–ASEAN Trade Weakens", *Xinhua News*, 20 July 2016, at <http://www.shanghaidaily.com/business/finance/Boom-in-ChinaASEAN-trade-weakens/shdaily.shtml> (accessed 20 July 2016).

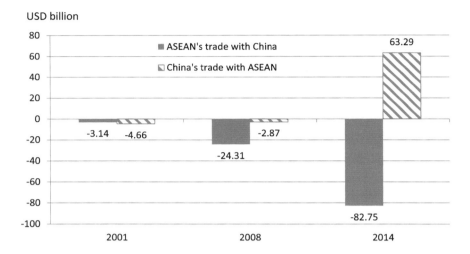

Figure 2. Trade Balances between China and ASEAN, 2001–2014

Sources: Calculated by the authors from International Monetary Fund, *Direction of Trade of ASEAN countries*; and CEIC Data Manager.

Second, bilateral trade has become increasingly unbalanced. According to data reported by ASEAN countries, the region had a relatively small trade deficit with China in 2001. The trade deficit rose sharply by 26% annually between 2001 and 2014. ASEAN's trade deficit with China amounted to US$83 billion in 2014 (Figure 2). Data from China shows that the country mostly had a trade deficit with ASEAN from 2001 to 2008. However, it reported trade surpluses of US$63.3 billion in 2014, roughly 13% of total bilateral trade. This emerging trade pattern suggests that ASEAN countries have become more closely tied to a China-centred regional production network and global supply chain as trade relations between China and ASEAN intensify. Although China's economy has grown significantly and its products globally competitive, together with its Asian neighbours, it continues to depend on consumers in the advanced economies for its exports and output.

Third, within ASEAN, China has increased its trade with the newer ASEAN members while the combined share of ASEAN's six older

Table 2. Share of Trade of ASEAN Members in China's Total Trade with ASEAN, 1997–2014 (%)

	1997	2001	2008	2014
Brunei	0.1	0.4	0.1	0.4
Indonesia	18.6	16.1	13.7	13.3
Malaysia	18.2	22.6	23.2	21.2
Philippines	6.8	8.5	12.4	9.3
Singapore	35.9	26.2	22.7	16.6
Thailand	14.5	17.3	17.8	15.1
Sub-total: ASEAN-6	94.1	91.0	89.8	75.9
Cambodia	—	0.6	0.5	0.8
Laos	—	0.1	0.2	0.8
Myanmar	—	1.5	1.1	5.2
Vietnam	5.9	6.7	8.4	17.4

Source: CEIC Data Manager.

members in China's trade had declined from 94% in 1997 to 76% in 2014. Within the six countries, Singapore saw the sharpest drop from 36% in 1997 to 17% in 2014. In 2008, Malaysia surpassed Singapore to become China's largest trading partner within ASEAN. In 2014, Vietnam overtook Singapore to become China's second-largest trading partner in ASEAN (Table 2). Between 1997 and 2014, the share of Indonesia in total China–ASEAN trade decreased from 19% to 13%. Meanwhile, the share of Malaysia, Philippines and Thailand increased between 1997 and 2008, but declined thereafter. Among ASEAN's four newer members, Cambodia, Laos, Myanmar and Vietnam, China's trade with Vietnam has grown the fastest. The share of China–Vietnam trade in total China–ASEAN trade increased from 6% in 1997 to 17% in 2014.

Malaysia has been China's largest trading partner among ASEAN members since 2008. Bilateral trade hit US$102 billion in 2014, a fivefold increase from that in 2003. Exports to and imports from China accounted for 12% and 17% of Malaysia's total, respectively (Table 3). Malaysia has consistently maintained a trade surplus with China. Machinery, electronics, plastic and fuels accounted for more than 50%

Table 3. ASEAN-6 Trade with China: Individual Countries' Exports (EX) to and Imports (IM) from China as a Proportion to Their Respective Total Exports and Imports (%)

	Brunei		Indonesia		Malaysia		Philippines		Singapore		Thailand		ASEAN	
	EX	IM	EX	IM	EX	IM	EX	IM	EX	IM	EX	IM	EX	IM
1985	—	2.0	0.5	2.4	1.0	2.0	1.8	5.4	1.4	8.6	3.8	2.4	1.3	5.0
1990	—	2.7	3.2	3.0	2.1	1.9	0.8	1.4	1.5	3.4	1.2	3.3	1.8	2.9
1995	—	3.0	3.8	3.7	2.6	2.2	1.2	2.3	2.3	3.2	2.8	2.7	2.7	3.1
2001	4.0	1.4	3.9	6.0	4.3	5.2	2.5	2.9	4.4	6.2	4.4	6.0	4.3	5.9
2007	3.1	5.6	8.5	11.5	8.8	12.9	11.4	7.2	9.7	12.1	9.6	11.6	9.2	12.6
2010	7.0	12.9	9.9	15.1	12.5	12.6	11.1	8.4	10.4	10.8	11.1	13.2	10.9	13.6
2012	2.7	21.3	11.4	15.3	12.6	15.1	11.8	10.8	10.8	10.3	11.7	14.9	11.4	14.8
2014	1.8	27.0	10.0	17.2	12.0	16.9	13.0	15.0	12.6	12.1	11.0	16.9	12.7	18.9

Source: Calculated by the authors from data obtained from International Monetary Fund, *Direction of Trade of ASEAN countries.*

of Malaysia's exports to China. Bilateral economic ties are expected to further strengthen.

Singapore was China's most important trading partner in ASEAN until 2008 when it was displaced by Malaysia and subsequently by Vietnam when it became China's top trading partner in 2014. In 2014, Singapore's exports to and imports from China accounted for 13% and 12% of Singapore's total, respectively. China's trade with Singapore recorded US$80 billion in 2014, over half of which constituted machinery and electrical products.[5] Nonetheless, Singapore remains significant to China as its second-largest market for exports and the third-largest source of imports within ASEAN.

Indonesia is ASEAN's most populous country, constituting more than 40% of ASEAN's population. China is Indonesia's top trading partner and total bilateral trade hit US$63.58 billion in 2014. Indonesia's exports to and imports from China in 2014 accounted for 10% and 17% of Indonesia's total with the world, respectively. China–Indonesia trade currently resembles the resources-for-manufactures pattern. More than half of Indonesia's imports from China are machinery and electronics, whereas energy, coal, raw materials and agricultural products make up three-quarters of Indonesia's exports to China, compared to 45% of its exports to the world.

Thailand is the second-largest economy in ASEAN. It is also highly export-oriented, with an export-to-GDP ratio of 65% in 2014. Thailand is not only an automobile manufacturing hub in the region, but also has a significant comparative advantage in agricultural products. In 2014, Thailand's exports to and imports from China made up 11% and 17% of the country's total exports and imports, respectively. Thailand's trade with China is quite distinctive. Machinery and electrical products, plastic or rubber, and chemicals accounted for two-thirds

---

[5] Nargiza Salidjanova, Iacob Koch-Weser and Jason Klanderman, "China's Economic Ties with ASEAN: A Country-by-Country Analysis", US–China Economic and Security Review Commission, 2015, p. 7, at <http://origin.www.uscc.gov/sites/default/files/Research/China's%20Economic%20Ties%20with%20ASEAN.pdf> (accessed 30 May 2016).

of Thai exports to China. A unique feature of Thai trade is the export of services, particularly tourism, which allows the country to have a positive trade surplus in term of goods and services with China.

Bilateral trade between China and Vietnam has developed strongly in recent years despite their territorial disputes in the South China Sea. Since 2003, Vietnam's trade with China has grown by 30% annually on average from US$4.64 billion in 2003 to US$84 billion in 2014. That said, China is Vietnam's largest trading partner. Vietnam ran a trade deficit of nearly US$44 billion with China in 2014, up from US$31.7 billion in 2013. In 2014, Vietnam's exports to and imports from China constituted 12% and 35% of its total, respectively. Vietnam mostly exports raw materials to China and imports manufactured products such as garment, equipment and machinery. Vietnam also imports large amount of electricity for the consumption in its northern provinces.[6]

Growing Investment Flows between China and ASEAN

Investment flows between China and ASEAN had increased considerably in recent years. More specifically, China's outbound direct investment (OFDI) has risen substantially since the early 2000s when a "going out" policy was initiated. Although a large majority of its OFDI went to Asia (69% in 2014), the amount to ASEAN remains relatively low. In 2014, a mere 6.3% of China's total FDI flowed into ASEAN. China's foreign direct investment (FDI) flow into ASEAN was only US$21 billion between 2003 and 2012 but more than doubled (US$48 billion) in 2014.

---

[6] The Electricity of Vietnam, the country's power utility, imports several billions of kilowatt-hour of electricity from China to ensure supply for 13 provinces in the north according to the Vietnam News Agency. See "Vietnam's Trade Deficit with China Widens to $5.17bn in Jan-Feb", Tuoi Tre News, 13 March 2015, at <http://tuoitrenews.vn/business/26720/vietnams-trade-deficit-with-china-widens-to-517bn-in-janfeb> (accessed 18 May 2016).

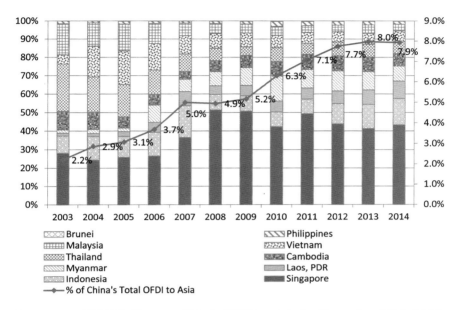

Figure 3. ASEAN's Share in China's OFDI to Asia by Countries, 2003–2014
Source: CEIC Data Manager.

In 2014, China's accumulated OFDI to ASEAN accounted for 7.9% of its total to Asia (Figure 3). Although the share seems relatively low, it represents a significant increase from about a mere 2.2% in 2003. China is a major investor in resource-rich countries in ASEAN, and its FDI remains significant in Cambodia, Laos and Myanmar. Based on China's reports on its accumulated OFDI as of 2014, Singapore is the largest recipient (about two-fifths of the total to the region) in ASEAN, followed by Indonesia (14%), Myanmar (8%), Laos (9%), Thailand (7%) and Vietnam (6%).

As China's OFDI to ASEAN increases, the structure of these investments has also changed. As of 2007, nearly a quarter of China's OFDI in ASEAN was in manufacturing. The other sectors that constitute the largest direct investment from China are "banking and insurance" (18% of total), "wholesale and retail trade" (15%) and "leasing and commercial service" (11%). Since then, between 2007 and 2013, mining and utilities sectors attracted larger amount of China's OFDI to the region, or 35% of the total. By 2013, the sectors in ASEAN that attracted the most FDI from China are "energy" (17%), "mining" (15%), "wholesale and retail trade" (13%), "manufacturing" (13%) and "leasing and commercial services" (11%).[7]

Singapore has long been an outlier in terms of investment flow between China and ASEAN as it receives the lion's share of Chinese FDI to the region. Chinese investors find Singapore relatively attractive as it is a global financial and logistic hub with more advantages in tariff concessions, and greater investment and intellectual property protection. For example, China's internet giant Alibaba invested US$1 billion in Lazada, a Singapore company that becomes the biggest e-retailer in Southeast Asia region in 2016. In fact, Alibaba has invested in Singapore Post (SingPost) and its logistic subsidiary, Quantum Solution which has more than 200 customers in 2014. China Construction Bank had also signed a memorandum of understanding with International Enterprise (IE) of Singapore to support Singapore and China companies involved in the "One Belt, One Road" project. Recently, China and Singapore companies jointly established Ispace Innovations Asia Pacific, an innovation centre in Singapore to attract more investors to participate in innovation businesses.

According to Control Risk's report, Chinese investment's in Indonesia in 2013 and 2014 mainly targeted at mining (34.8%), energy (21.4%), and construction (19.6%).[8] Since 2013, China has invested nearly US$5 billion in energy sector, about US$3 billion in construction sector and US$1 billion in mining sector. The Chinese government is keen to speed up railway construction and local port upgrading in Indonesia. For example, Chinese–Indonesian consortium, Kereta Cepat Indonesia China (KCIC), won the tender to build Indonesia's Jakarta–Bandung railway construction in October 2015, mainly because they could provide the cheaper high-speed rail project

---

[7] The figures are based on CEIC Data Manager.
[8] "Chinese Investment in Indonesia", *Indonesia Newsletter, Control Risk*, no. 2, August 2015, at <https://controlrisks.com/en/newsletters/indonesia-newsletter/issue-2/chinese-investment-in-indonesia> (accessed 5 January 2017).

for Indonesia government. In addition, China is accountable for Indonesia's increased mining activities in nickel ore to make stainless steel, jet engine and so on.

In recent years, Malaysia has many investment projects with China, mainly in infrastructure, real estate construction and manufacturing sectors. According to official data, China's manufacturing investments in Malaysia reached about RM13.6 billion (about US$3.1 billion) between 2009 and 2015.[9] Chinese companies preferred to invest in industries that promote the economic growth objective of Malaysia Plan such as basic metal, electronics and electrical, textiles and non-metallic minerals. Ongoing projects that emerge as China's hot investments are China–Kuantan Industrial Park, Malacca Gateway project, Penang reclamation project and Malaysia City project. The Singapore–Kuala Lumpur high-speed railway project is currently one of the priorities of China's outward direct investment.

As is shown in Figure 3, China's investment in Cambodia, Laos, Myanmar and Vietnam has significantly increased, even though the percentage share is still low. China mainly invested in infrastructure construction and processing manufacturing. For instance, many companies in Yunnan province had projects in Laos that involve road enhancement, and generation of electricity and water supplies. China and Laos also made concerted effort to build a cross-border economic zone to support free trade agreement projects. Chinese companies continue to move their factories, particularly those in low-end processing manufacturing sector such as textile industry, to Vietnam in order to cut cost, despite the uncertainty in relationship between both countries.

On the other hand, ASEAN's direct investment to China has also been growing in recent years, albeit at a slower rate. China's total utilised FDI from ASEAN amounted to US$6.3 billion in 2014, of which 92% originated from Singapore (US$5.8 billion), and the

---

[9] "China Investments to Lift Malaysia's Outlook", *The Star Online*, 17 April 2016, at <http://www.thestar.com.my/news/nation/2016/04/17/china-investments-to-lift-malaysias-outlook/> (accessed 5 January 2017).

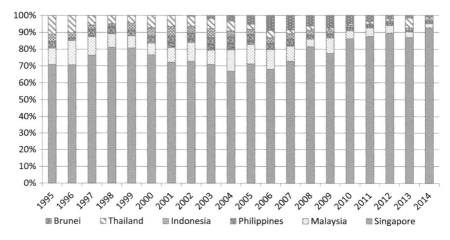

Figure 4. China's Utilised FDI from ASEAN-6, 1995–2014
Source: CEIC Data Manager.

remaining were from Malaysia and Indonesia. Overall, between 2000 and 2014, Singapore contributed over four-fifths of total ASEAN-6's FDI in China, and Malaysia was a distant second, contributing just 7.3% of ASEAN-6's investment in China (Figure 4). Significantly, Singapore's utilised FDI to China in ASEAN-6 had grown in strength during the global economic slowdown when other ASEAN-6 countries performed weaker in outward direct investment.

Singapore companies are shifting their investment focus from China's coastal regions to inland regions, such as Chengdu and Chongqing. The third government-to-government project, China–Singapore (Chongqing) Demonstration Initiative on Strategic Connectivity which focused on modern connectivity and services, was signed in September 2014. Singapore's edge in financial services is beneficial to this initiative, i.e. in exploring China's market and reaping economic benefits from its growing economy. The China–Singapore Suzhou Industrial Park and Tianjin Eco-city are previous proofs of successful collaboration between both countries. Singapore wants to create value-add to developments in the western region by enhancing connectivity within the region as well as to other parts of China and the world.

Challenges to Strengthening Bilateral Economic Relations

Since the 1980s, China–ASEAN bilateral economic relations have gradually but substantially enhanced, especially in the areas of trade and direct investment. Such strong and resilient linkages have not only facilitated the development of China and ASEAN member states, but also helped to sustain the growth momentum and promote economic integration in East and Southeast Asia, most significantly since the late 1990s. Bilateral economic relations are set to strengthen further. In addition to trade and direct investment, bilateral economic ties can take on many other forms, including tourism, trade in services, financial cooperation, official aid and various joint projects. ASEAN's diverse cultural heritage has promoted the region as one of the most attractive destinations for both regional and international tourists.

Tourism cooperation between China and ASEAN has also developed rapidly in recent years and become an important component in trade in services. As the Chinese middle class with stronger purchasing power seeks more exotic travelling experiences, tourism is likely to be an imperative source of revenue for ASEAN countries, particularly Thailand. In 2014, according to the latest available data, around 13 million Chinese tourists travelled to ASEAN, the second-largest tourist group to ASEAN countries which accounted for 12.4% of ASEAN's total tourism.[10]

China has also increased its economic cooperation with ASEAN countries in the form of outward contracted projects, which were valued at US$17 billion in 2013, up from US$1.5 billion in 2002. In the coming decades, China aims to transform its economy through further integration of its economy with the rest of the world, especially Southeast Asia. ASEAN countries also aspire to develop through better intraregional and interregional economic integration. That said, China

---

[10] Association of Southeast Asian Nations, "Top Ten Country/Regional Sources of Visitors to ASEAN", 30 September 2015, at <http://www.asean.org/storage/2015/11/tourism/Table_30.pdf> (accessed 5 January 2017).

and ASEAN — two large, diverse and dynamic economies — could reap huge benefit through closer trade and investment relations.

More significantly, China is committed to further improving its relations with its neighbours through collaboration in its initiatives like the 21st-Century Maritime Silk Road initiative, AIIB and Silk Road Fund. China and ASEAN are likely to become a strong driving force for regional development and infrastructure construction. Improvements to regional connectivity and accessibility will boost ASEAN's economy.

As ASEAN countries are increasingly dependent on the Chinese market for their exports, China's recent deceleration in growth may have a chain effect on some ASEAN countries. Similarly, China's imports from its neighbours may be affected by uncertainties in the global economy. Meanwhile, as China's economy grows and its influence in the region increases, mistrust between both sides has deepened. From the perspective of some ASEAN states, a large and strong neighbour is naturally threatening. From China's perspective, the inducement of an outside power, such as the United States, into the region exhibits hostile intentions.

Such mutual suspicion means progress could be slow and arduous. For example, lacking in concrete details, it is unclear how China's Silk Road initiatives could work well with ASEAN's intraregional development plans. Similarly, it will take time for the AIIB to function as an effective supplement to the existing global financial architecture for Asia's infrastructure construction.

China–ASEAN bilateral relations are tainted by potential flashpoints, such as the South China Sea conflict, besides economic uncertainties and mistrust between China and some ASEAN member states. Notwithstanding the complex and long-standing nature of the problems, any serious mishandling could sabotage the Chinese government's years of efforts and derail bilateral economic relations.

Chapter 7

Ever-Bonding Sino–Korean Economic Relationship but Questionable Contribution to Regional Integration

CHOO Jaewoo*

The relation between the People's Republic of China (PRC, thereafter China) and the Republic of Korea (ROK, thereafter Korea or South Korea) is one outstanding example of the "Asian Paradox" at work. Their political and security relationship, however, does not commensurate the growing economic relations. Both countries do not appear to have found a way to build much political confidence and trust in each other. A number of theories argue that there should be some degree of correlation in the relationship as one party is supposed to have some so-called "spillover" effects into the other. Such argument was first introduced as early as in 1795 in Immanuel Kant's essay "Perpetual Peace: A Philosophical Sketch".[1] The premise of perpetual peace is the assimilation of cosmopolitanism in areas such as thinking, values, institutions and eventually systems. The idea was further developed and evolved into the theory of interdependence.

---

* Choo Jaewoo is Professor of Chinese foreign policy in the Department of Chinese Studies at Kyung Hee University, Republic of Korea.
[1] Immanuel Kant, *Perpetual Peace and Other Essays*, translated by Ted Humphrey, Indianapolis, IN, Hackett Publishing Company, 1992, pp. 107–126.

Thereafter, trade-fostering peace has become the main theme of liberalism.[2] Although it is not evident economy has positive effects on politics in the development of Sino–Korean bilateral relationship, the negative effects, if any, have precluded wars or direct physical confrontations. On the contrary, both sides "allow" conflicts of interest and ensuing diplomatic challenges to arise. These challenges will hence fundamentally hinder the two countries' progress on the economic front and ultimately impede their goal realisation to achieve and contribute positively to regional economic integration of Northeast Asia.

China and Korea are therefore under the illusion that their growing economic relations have positive spillover effects on regional economic integration. On what basis do China and Korea derive their argument? It is difficult to identify a valid supporting reason to the argument if one were to analyse and study the subject in greater depth. While some analyses attribute the reason to the growing regional economic interdependence as a natural consequence, others attribute the reason to the artificial construct of regional institutions by the regional states. Growing interdependence through increased intraregional trade, the ever-deepening of division of labour, and the expanding economic network normally facilitate economies towards integration. However, the reality proves otherwise, as the security predicament of these regional economies appears to impede integration. Recent developments in the new security predicaments have undermined the foundation of institutions built for Northeast Asian economic integration.

---

[2] Geoffrey Blainey, *The Cause of War*, New York, NY, Free Press, 1973; James D Fearon, "Domestic Political Audiences and the Escalation of International Disputes", *American Political Science Review*, vol. 88, no. 3, 1994, pp. 577–592; Katherine Barbieri and Gerald Schneider, "Globalization and Peace: Assessing New Directions in the Study of Trade and Conflict", *Journal of Peace Research*, vol. 36, no. 4, 1999, pp. 387–404; John R Oneal and Bruce M Russett, "The Classical Liberals Were Right: Democracy, Interdependence, and Conflict, 1950–1985", *International Studies Quarterly*, vol. 41, no. 2, 1997, pp. 267–293; John R Oneal and Bruce M Russett, "Assessing the Liberal Peace with Alternative Specifications: Trade Still Reduces Conflict", *Journal of Peace Research*, vol. 36, no. 4, 1999, pp. 423–442; and Harrison R Wagner, "Bargaining and War", *American Journal of Political Science*, vol. 44, no. 3, 2000, pp. 469–484.

The prospect of holding China–Japan–Korea (CJK) trilateral summit in November 2016 was dramatically dimmed and affected by the recent political developments between China and Korea, after the latter decided in July 2016 to deploy Terminal High Altitude Area Defence (THAAD) system to the former's dismay. The CJK summit in 2015 was finally held in November in Seoul after a hiatus of three and a half years due to political conflicts between China and Japan, and between Japan and Korea pertaining to territorial disputes and to historical issues about comfort women, respectively. Political conflicts, if they arise in this region, seem to have the capacity to change mindset of regional economies about economic cooperation, thereby marginalising the benefits of cooperation. In Northeast Asia where politics still dictates economics, confrontation appears to be an affordable challenge in the region. Security and political interests indeed prevail over interests engendered by economic cooperation. To economies which uphold and regard national self-esteem and national dignity as top priority, any negative impacts on economic cooperation and integration as a result of confrontation are tolerable.

It appeared that a diplomatic rift in China–Korea bilateral relationship was going to be an obstacle to realising the CJK summit in November 2016. However, it turned out to be Korea's domestic political turmoil that eventually led to the impeachment process for President Park's scandal that broke out in October and to the infinite postponement of the summit. Even if the summit was held, the prospect of integration will not be optimistic, largely because China–Korea bilateral relationship would be strained upon the completion of THAAD deployment. The bilateral relations will remain strained even after deployment because THAAD in itself not only poses a threat to China's national security interest but is also a source of security dilemma with serious strategic implications for all regional players including the United States. This subsequently only perpetuates a divide between the aimers (i.e. the United States, Korea and Japan) and the targets or the threatened (i.e. North Korea, China and Russia) that will eventually deprive the nations of an opportunity to build the requisite confidence and trust towards regional economic integration.

Given the bleak prospect of Sino–Korean bilateral relations and regional economic integration, this chapter offers a short-term, albeit largely pessimistic, analysis of Sino–Korean relationship and the progress of regional economic integration. However, the pessimism turned around with leadership change in Korea in mid-2017 due to President Park's impeachment and with the advent of Chinese President Xi Jinping's second term.[3] The turnaround was realised by the fruition of the CJK summit which was held in Tokyo in May 2018.

Taken from this perspective, this chapter will first review the evolution of Sino–Korean economic relations in recent times. The second section analyses China's recent aggressive act towards security-related issues of Korea, which will explain the cause of rift in the bilateral relationship. The third section concludes with some prospective studies on the short-term impact of the rift on regional economic cooperation progress and beyond.

The Ever-Expanding Sino–Korean Economic Ties

Bilateral trade between China and Korea took a quantum leap from US$5.2 billion in 1992 to US$134 billion in 2006, with an average annual growth of 20%. At that rate, China displaced the United States in 2004 as Korea's biggest trading partner. It was intriguing that the bilateral trade volume reached the US$100 billion mark in 2005, only two years after having surpassed US$50 billion, and it would break the US$200 billion mark in 2012, doubling the volume in only seven years. Likewise, China and South Korea enjoy robust bilateral investment relations with rapid annual growth in recent years. China is the largest overseas investment destination for Korea, while Korea is the fifth-largest investor in China, discounting tax havens such as the Caribbean states and transit economies like Hong Kong. Growing bilateral economic relations have also facilitated immigration of

---

[3] Lim Wen Xin, "Xi Jinping and China's Future: A Debate", *IPP Review*, 1 August 2016, at <http://ippreview.com/index.php/Home/Blog/single/id/204.html> (accessed 3 August 2016).

Koreans to China and vice versa. There are currently more than 800,000 Koreans and 58,000 Korean students in China. Korean students are by far the largest group of foreign students studying in China. Conversely, more than a million Chinese now live and work in Korea, and there are more than 60,000 Chinese students studying in Korea.

After the normalisation of ties in 1992, Korea's exports to China rose from US$2.65 billion the same year to US$145.33 billion, an increase of 54.8 folds. Korea's imports from China also grew dramatically by 24.2 folds from US$3.72 billion in 1992 to US$90.07 billion in 2014. Over the same period, the share of China in Korea's total export market increased from 3.5% to 25.4%; the share of China in Korea's total import market also grew from 3.5% to 17.1%. As a result, with increased total trade volume from US$6.37 billion in 1992 to US$235.4 billion in 2014, China became Korea's largest trading partner. It is noteworthy that Korea's total trade with China is larger than the combined total trade with the United States and Japan (US$201.5 billion).[4]

Similarly, as bilateral ties normalised, China's export to Korea increased 41.7 folds from US$2.4 billion in 1992 to US$100.33 billion in 2014. China's import from Korea also increased from US$2.62 billion in 1992 to US$190.11 billion in 2014, recording a 72.5-fold increase.[5]

In 2014, as Korea's share in China's total trade rose from 3.3% to 9.7%, Korea thus became China's largest import market. Korea is currently China's fourth-largest export market after a steady growth from 2.8% to 4.3% of its total export share over the same period.

In terms of investment, China is the second-largest destination of Korea's foreign direct investment, registering an annual average investment growth of US$2.9 billion from 1992 to 2015. Korea's accumulative total investment in China over the 1992–2015 period amounted

---

[4] Lee Buhyung and Chun Yongchang, *Issues and Challenges: Importance of Korea–China Economic Relationship and Ways Forward*, Seoul, Hyundai Economic Research Institute, 9 March 2016, p. 3.
[5] Lee and Chun, *Issues and Challenges*, p. 4.

to US$69.71 billion, only second to the United States at US$87.95 billion. From 2002 to 2014, Korea's total accumulative investment in China rose 16 folds from US$3.86 billion to US$61.85 billion, accounting for 13.7% of its total foreign direct investment.[6]

China was the eighth-largest investor in Korean economy with an accumulated investment of US$8.11 billion in value from 2002 to 2014. However, China's investment in Korea has dramatically risen in recent years. From 2002 to 2014, Chinese investment in Korea increased by 14.8 times from US$2.58 billion to US$38.21 billion.[7] In 2015 alone, Chinese investment hovered around US$4.03 billion, almost half of accumulative amount as of 2014. The total volume marked the fourth-largest amount in 2015. From 1995 to 2015, in terms of cumulative investment, China was the fifth-largest investor in Korean market. As is evident, Chinese investment in Korea was marginal during the first three years after normalisation of relations in 1992. Chinese investment now makes up about 4.7% of Korea's total inward investment.

People-to-people exchange has witnessed a dramatic growth in recent times. In 2014, the total number of Korea-bound Chinese visitors and China-bound Korean visitors surpassed 10 million people for the first time since relations were normalised. This number totalled 10.59 million people in 2015, with 6.154 million Chinese visiting South Korea and 4.444 million South Koreans travelling to China. This also registered an increase of 80 folds when comparing the 130,000 mutual visits made in total in 1992 — the year bilateral diplomatic relations normalised — to 10.59 million visits in 2015. As of 2016, there were 1,250 flights per week on 97 routes between both countries, of which 450 flights per week were between Korea and Shanghai.

On the tourism front, Chinese visitors to Korea increased 33.6 folds from 178,000 in 1995 to 5.98 million in 2015. They accounted for 45.2% of total foreigners visiting Korea, and generated

---

[6] Lee and Chun, *Issues and Challenges*, p. 8.
[7] Lee and Chun, *Issues and Challenges*.

US$9.96 billion in tourism earnings for Korea, approximately 55.8% of its total tourism earnings (US$17.48 billion) in 2014. Conversely, South Korea is China's fourth-largest source of foreign visitors. In 1995, there were 530,000 Korean visitors to China and the number increased 8.4 folds to 4.44 million Korean visitors in 2015. Korean visitors spent US$2.14 billion in China in 2014, accounting for 3.7% of China's total tourist earnings.

The total trade between South Korea and China was widely predicted to break the US$300 billion mark in 2015, with the conclusion of the South Korea–China free trade agreement in 2013 which took effect in 2015. Instead, total trade declined from US$235.4 billion in 2014 to US$227.3 billion in 2015, registering a decrease of 3.4%. For the first time since 1992, bilateral trade decreased for two consecutive years.[8] With security and political challenges looming large following South Korea's announcement of its decision to deploy THAAD on 8 July, it is widely speculated that Chinese punitive economic measures will further hinder the growth of trade and investment relations between China and Korea in the near future.

A Diplomatic Rift: Political and Security Challenges

Chinese and Korean analysts tend to adopt contrasting approaches in their studies of bilateral relations. Chinese, whether inadvertently or not, show a propensity to eschew thorny political issues in their studies, unless the topic is related to politics-specific. Hence, most, if not all, Chinese literature usually renders positive aspects of the bilateral developments. The Chinese only become critical of the bilateral relationship

---

[8] Li Mengmeng, "Breaking News on 2015 Korea — Trade Relations", *Global Window*, Beijing, KOTRA, 26 February 2016, available at <http://www.globalwindow.org/GW/global/trade/economy-trend/overseamarket-detail.html?MENU_CD=M10015&SCH_TYPE=SCH_SJ&MODE=L&SCH_CMMDY_CATE_CD=00000&SCH_TRADE_CD=0000000&UPPER_MENU_CD=M10003&NM_KO=&BBS_ID=10&NM_EN=&SCH_VALUE=&MENU_STEP=2&SCH_AREA_CD=00000&Page=1&SCH_NATION_CD=000000&SCH_START_DT=&BKCODE=&RowCountPerPage=10&SCH_END_DT=&ARTICLE_ID=5035776> (accessed 23 June 2016).

when specific issues pertaining to North Korea and sometimes in the context of the South Korea's relations with the United States require China to respond firmly.[9]

The Koreans, on the other hand, attempt to take a more balanced approach by analysing achievements and challenges. Korea, being on the periphery of China, needs to be more sensitive to and conscious of the China factor while defending its national interests. Korea is not exempt from the impact of China's rise and China's muscular diplomatic endeavours. China's assertive and aggressive actions have, therefore, precipitated Korea's China threat perception.

Another factor that Korea's analyses often taken into account is China's alliance relationship with the North. South Korea has blind faith and expectation in China to assume a constructive role in mediating crises or conflicts aroused by the North. Hence, Korean observers are concerned about the intent behind China's "charm offensive" and its seemingly unilateral decision in denying South Korea's historic and sovereign rights to defend territorial and security interests. However, China's charm offensive and economic opportunities, which the Koreans recognise with appreciation, present a controversial paradox in the nexus between security and economy.[10]

Sino–South Korean relations, rife with challenges, have never been smooth sailing since both countries established formal diplomatic ties on 24 August 1992. As Chinese experts focus on economic statistics, deepening China–Korea economic interdependence, and growing exchanges and collaborations in various areas in their analyses, they have not adequately addressed the challenges on political, diplomatic and

---

[9] A salient example of this sort of literary work is Liu Baocai, "Quzhe dongdang de yi nian: 2010 nian guoji xingshi huimou" (A Distorted and Rocky Year — Reflection on the Developments in International Relations in 2010), *Hongqi wengao* (Beijing: *Qiushi* Journal), no. 1, 2011, at <http://www.qstheory.cn/hqwg/2011/201101/201101/t20110111_61809.htm> (accessed 23 March 2011).
[10] Kim Taeho, "Sino-ROK Relations at 15: An Overview and Assessment", *CAPS Working Paper Series*, no. 5, 1 August 2007, at <http://commons.ln.edu.hk/capswp/5?utm_source=commons.ln.edu.hk%2Fcapswp%2F5&utm_medium=PDF&utm_campaign=PDFCoverPages> (accessed 23 June 2016).

security fronts — i.e. the North Korean factor — for political reasons. Hence, North Korean provocations and their impacts on Sino–South Korean bilateral relations are seldom discussed. Furthermore, there is a lack of confidence- and trust-building opportunities between China and South Korea to develop effective partnership on political and security fronts.

Besides, the fact that China and South Korea had let slip the opportunities to build political confidence and trust between them implies that both sides face obstacles in advancing their sanguine economic cooperative relationship towards regional economic integration. Both countries, in fact, have a good relationship, better than their respective relationship with Japan. Had the two had success in achieving a certain level of mutual confidence and trust, they would have achieved regional integration with full participation from Japan, which, assumedly a rational actor, would not want to be left out of the regional integration.

Notwithstanding China's and South Korea's politically hostile relations with Japan, a rift in fact emerged in Sino–South Korean bilateral relations in recent years. The rift was caused by a third party, not as a result of conflict of interest or direct rivalry. North Korea's provocations in 2010 include the sinking of South Korea's Cheonan vessel on 26 March, the shelling of Yeonpyeong Island on 23 November and the United States' subsequent decision to conduct a series of punitive joint military exercises (25 to 28 July and 28 November to 1 December) aroused Beijing.

Several events resulted in political rift in China's relations with South Korea: on 20 May 2010, China took a partisan posture, ignoring the International Joint Investigation Committee's verdict on North Korea as the main culprit of the sinking;[11] and on 22 June, China issued first warning to Korea and the United States not to conduct military

---

[11] The Joint Civilian-Military Investigation Group, "Investigation Result on the Sinking of ROKS 'Cheonan'", 20 May 2010, at <http://nautilus.org/wp-content/uploads/2012/01/Cheonan.pdf> (accessed 22 May 2010).

exercises on its "own waters".[12] South Korea grew increasingly sceptical of China's peaceful rise after China defined and claimed Korea's territorial waters as its own backyard.[13] On the shelling incident, China, in an act of political partisanship, sided with North Korea, arguing that the shelling was an act of self-defence since South Korea disregarded the North's warnings of no live firing.[14] China's defence of North Korea was widely regarded as biased, unjust and blatant defiance because the North's "retaliation" act of firing artillery rounds on the Yeonpyeong Island that resulted in casualties, including deaths of two civilians and two marines, was not merely an intent of deterrence.[15]

---

[12] Evans Revere, "A Dragon Rises: China's Ascendancy and US–ROK Relationship", paper presented at Center for US–Korea Policy workshop, Jeju, Korea, August 2010, at <https://asiafoundation.org/resources/pdfs/2.EvansREVERE.pdf> (accessed 22 June 2016). Some Chinese generals made forceful assertions in their statement. Chinese Navy General Yin Zhuo emphasised the fact from Chinese perspective that there had never been a "middle line" (neutral line, *zhongjianxian*) in the Yellow Sea, and hence, such exercises in the Yellow Sea "threaten" the security of economic development in Chinese coastal areas and are considered unfriendly actions. General Yin also declared that Chinese military was not afraid of it. "Wo jun shaojiang cheng mei hangmu bushu Huanghai xu 24 xiaoshi, wo jun bu weiju" (Our Rear Admiral Claims US Aircraft Carrier Needs 24 Hours for Deployment, and Our Military is Not Afraid), *Huanqiu shibao (Global Times)*, 7 July 2010. Other generals like Ma Xiaotian (the deputy chief of the General Staff of the PLA), and Luo Yuan (deputy secretary-general of Military Science Society Major General) also expressed similar concerns.

[13] China perceived the United States' and South Korea's joint military exercise with deployment of USS George Washington as an "intrusion" and "expansion" into waters near China. Chinese Foreign Ministry Spokesperson's Press Briefing on July 8, 2010, at <http://www.fmprc.gov.cn/chn/gxh/tyb/fyrbt/jzhsl/t714888.htm> (accessed 11 July 2010). Studies on Korea's perceptual change of China's rise following two incidents, see Kim Jiyoon and Woo Jung-yup, *Report on the Survey Regarding the Yeonpyeong Shelling Incident*, (Seoul: Asian Institute for Policy Studies, November 2010), p. 18; and Pew Research Center, *America's Global Image Remains More Positive than China's*, 18 July 2013, Ch. 3.

[14] Shen Dingli, "Ending the Tension", *www.china.org*, 27 November 2010; and Shen Dingli, "International Cooperation for Peace in the Korean Peninsula", paper presented at the international conference on Crisis on the Korean Peninsula and Peace-Making, Seoul, 18 April 2011.

[15] "China, Russia Side with N. Korea", *Dong-A Ilbo*, 20 December 2010.

Since 2010, Beijing has kept up its extreme displeasure with South Korea's resultant military manoeuvres directed at its assertive defensive measures and at North Korea's provocations. China made a unilateral and sudden declaration of its air defence identification zone on 23 November 2013 that extended to overlap with that of Korea's and Japan's.[16] Beijing's decision, whether intentional or not, to extend the zone overlapping with that of others only heightens the geopolitical challenges of the region. Since the United States began the conceptualisation of deploying Terminal High Altitude Area Defence (THAAD) system to its military base in South Korea, Beijing has been outspoken of its opposition, attacking South Korea's sovereign rights to national defence as a violation of China's sovereign rights. China's warning to South Korea of a breakdown in bilateral ties in the event of THAAD deployment was considered a "blackmail" by South Korea.[17] Following Korea's announcement of its decision on 8 July 2016 to deploy THAAD, some Chinese critics asserted that Korea's THAAD site(s) would inevitably become vulnerable target of China's surgical strike, should a conflict occur between China and the United States and its allies.[18]

---

[16] On the contrary, China claimed that it was South Korea which first expanded and intruded to overlap its air defence identification zone (ADIZ). Zhang Yiqian, "Seoul Expands KADIZ South", *Global Times*, 9 December 2013. However, the chronology of the announcements by the two countries refuted Chinese claim. China first expanded to include Korea's territorial areas in its ADIZ on 23 November, and in response, Korea announced on 8 December to expand its ADIZ to protect the areas effectively from 15 December. Kang Seung-Woo, "Korea Includes Ieodo, Hongdo, Marado in Air Defense Zone", *The Korea Times*, 8 December 2015. Adopting a diplomatic resolve to peacefully settle the issue through dialogues, Korea demanded China to adjust its ADIZ but only to be rejected at the Defense Strategic Dialogue. Song Sang-ho, "Beijing Rejects Seoul's Call for Adjustment of its Air Zone", *The Korea Times*, 28 November 2013.

[17] Shin Hyun-hee, "China Envoy Warns of 'Destruction' of Ties Due to THAAD", *The Korea Herald*, 23 February 2016; and Jack Kim, "South Korea, U.S. to Deploy THAAD Missile Defense, Drawing China Rebuke", *The Reuters*, 8 July 2016, at <http://www.reuters.com/article/us-southkorea-usa-thaad-idUSKCN0ZO084> (accessed 9 July 2016).

[18] Ding Gang, "THAAD Can be Target of Surgical Strike", *Global Times*, 20 July 2016.

Ironically two of the three defence-related conflicts between China and Korea happened when the CJK summit hit a stalemate. In between conflicts, newly elected leaders in Beijing and Seoul attempted to mend the relationship. Xi Jinping decided to visit South Korea first, skipping North Korea, while South Korean President Park Geun-hye attended the military parade on 3 September 2015 held in Beijing in commemoration of China's 70th Anniversary of Victory over Japan and the end of World War II, despite much opposition from Washington.[19] It was alleged that China's decision to attend the CJK summit held in Seoul on 1 November 2015 was made in reciprocation of Park's attendance at China's 70th anniversary V-Day military parade. However, Park's decision to deploy THAAD had put the seemingly close ties between China and South Korea back to square one. This, coupled with her indictment process, postponed indefinitely the CJK summit originally scheduled to be held in Tokyo in November 2016.

The Chinese Communist Party and the Chinese government were vocal about China's opposition to the THAAD deployment on numerous occasions through various channels. This would culminate when Xi's explicit remarks in the face of President Obama at the Nuclear Security Summit in Washington on 31 March 2016 spoke volumes of China's vehement opposition to the deployment.[20] If the CJK summit were not to be held in Tokyo in 2016 — and on an annual regular basis thereafter, as it was compromised in 2015 — therefore, when the summit would have been held for the first time after three years of hiatus, it remains to be seen if the promise will be kept despite the reaffirmed commitment of the leaders of the three countries to do so.[21]

---

[19] David Nakamura, "South Korea–China Thaw may Complicate Obama's China Strategy", *The Stripes*, 15 October 2015, at <http://www.stripes.com/news/pacific/south-korea-china-thaw-may-complicate-obama-s-china-strategy-1.373539> (accessed 22 October 2015).
[20] "Xi Warns Obama against Threatening China's Sovereignty & National Interests", *The RT*, 1 April 2016, at <https://www.rt.com/news/337975-xi-obama-sovereignty-national-interests/> (accessed 2 April 2016).
[21] "Full Text of Joint Declaration of Trilateral Summit", *Yeonhap News*, 1 November 2015, at <http://english.yonhapnews.co.kr/national/2015/11/01/0301000000 AEN20151101003900315.html> (accessed 2 July 2016).

Prospects for China–Japan–Korea Trilateral Summit and Northeast Asian Regionalism

If China–Japan–Korea trilateral relations are seen as an analogy for a three-legged stool, all three legs appear to be independent of each other and too far apart to support the weight of Northeast Asian regionalism. Before Korea made the decision to deploy THAAD which caused a serious rift in Sino–Korean relations, the strength of the stool was sustained by the strong relations between both countries. The rift, however, has driven a wedge in the bilateral relations, resulting in imminent collapse of the tripod/stool. Korea's security decision is regarded as the critical factor that eventually cancelled the trilateral summit scheduled in Tokyo in November 2016. The trilateral summit held in 2015 was in fact resumed on a fragile foundation. It materialised because of US mediation of the strained relationship between Korea and Japan and Korea's bold decision to attend China's military parade despite US opposition.

Although the three countries pledged to hold their trilateral meet annually at the 2015 summit, prevailing short-term political impediments have make such a prospect bleak. As China retaliates Korea's announcement of THAAD to be operationalised by end of 2017 with punitive measures, tensions have built up in their bilateral relations. In this context, the three countries are unlikely to congregate for the summit in 2017 and beyond. The long-standing territorial disputes between China and Japan will further weaken the prospect of holding the trilateral summit. However, Korea and Japan's relations may be on the verge of recovery with an agreement reached on the comfort women issue in December 2015. Nonetheless, Korea and Japan's efforts in reconciling issues between them will not induce China to join the summit simply because China adopts an unyielding political posture, and also Japan and Korea are unwilling to make any compromise on the issues.

The only hope for the trilateral summit and for regional cooperation and economic integration to advance may lie in the changes of leadership. While leaders in China and Japan have remained intact, Korea has a new leader in office by the summer of 2017 as the impeachment of President Park was upheld by the court in March, thereby leading to an early presidential election in May 2017. With newly elected President Moon Jae-in coming into power, he certainly fulfilled expectations to bring about new policy changes and approaches to Korea's relationship with China. If such a change entailed a new posture in foreign policy whereby a compromise on the issues that set the two countries apart becomes viable, then, an improvement in the relationship would ensue as Korea maintains its "three no's" agreement made with China in October 2017.[22] With an improved relationship, a fresh start for the trilateral summit was convened as evident in the success of the CJK meeting held in May 2018.

---

[22] By accepting the so-called "three no's", South Korea agreed there would be no further anti-ballistic missile systems in Korea, no participation in a regionwide US missile defence system and no military alliance involving Korea, the United States and Japan; see "China Wins Its Wars against South Korea's US THAAD Missile Shields — Without Firing a Shot", *South China Morning Post*, 18 November 2017.

Chapter 8

China and Japan: Great Economic Integration without a Bilateral Free Trade Agreement

XING Yuqing*

With regionalism on the rise, countries and governments actively seek to promote trade and strengthen strategic relations with their neighbours or countries that are of geopolitical importance to them by forging and signing bilateral and multilateral free trade agreements (FTAs). Hence, in the last decade, Asia has seen dramatic growth and proliferation of FTAs. According to the Asian Development Bank, as of 2016, there are 226 FTAs in Asia — 147 are already in effect and the rest are under negotiation. China and Japan are two leading participants in the race of negotiating FTAs in Asia with their major trading or strategically important partners. China today has concluded 16 bilateral and multilateral FTAs while Japan has signed 15 FTAs.

There is no doubt that FTAs can lower trade barriers to a certain extent, and thus facilitate trade flows as well as enhance economic integration. Theoretically speaking, countries in close proximity to each other and with complementary economic structure would benefit

---

*XING Yuqing is Professor of Economics at the National Graduate Institute for Policy Studies in Japan.

much more from the FTA than countries that are far away from one another and have similar economic structures. In the case of China and Japan, the former is a developing country while the latter had long achieved industrialisation. Being neighbours, this implies that the transportation costs of trade flows between China and Japan are relatively low. However, both sides have not yet initiated negotiation of bilateral FTA. Both Japan and China are members of the World Trade Organisation (WTO), which entitles them the most favoured nation trading status. There is no other institutional arrangement that promotes Sino–Japanese bilateral trade. Worse still, political tensions and national security concerns have occasionally undermined the progress of FTA negotiations in which both China and Japan are involved, e.g. the China–Japan–Korea FTA and the Regional Comprehensive Economic Partnership (RCEP), which includes 10 ASEAN countries plus China, Japan, Korea, Australia, New Zealand and India.

Despite the unfavourable external environment, economic integration between China and Japan has progressed steadily. An invisible hand has closely guided and brought the two economies together. Since 2004, China has replaced the United States and emerged as the largest market of Japanese exports. Japan, on the other hand, has constantly been the second-largest market of Chinese exports. Sino–Japanese bilateral trade amounted to US$270 billion in 2015. In fact, Japanese firms had cumulatively invested more than US$100 billion in China. Even though Japanese firms scaled down their investments in China in recent years, China remains the largest destination of Japanese foreign direct investment (FDI) in Asia. Furthermore, the drastic surge of Chinese tourists in Japan and their buying frenzy are deemed the saviour of Japanese retailers, which have been struggling with shrinking domestic demand for decades. Massive cross-border flows of trade, investment and tourists have resulted in greater economic integration between China and Japan — a clear indication that economic motivations of both Chinese and Japanese consumers and firms have driven economic cooperation. The political tensions and diplomatic turmoil between China and Japan may occasionally slow down, but will not reverse, the trend of economic integration. This chapter provides a detailed account of the evolution of

Sino–Japanese economic integration in the past decades, focusing on trade, investment and tourism.

Sino–Japanese Bilateral Trade: Asia's Largest

Cross-country movements of goods, capital and labours are three fundamental factors that are conducive to linking economies in various geographic locations. Since 1990, bilateral trade has gradually led to the integration of and significant interdependence of China's and Japan's economy. Trade liberalisation under the umbrella of the WTO, of which both China and Japan are members and are entitled the status of the "most favoured" nations, had significantly promoted trade flows between the two countries. China's trade promotion policies, such as value-added tax rebate, tariff exemption on intermediate inputs used in manufacturing for exports, processing zones and so on, had also facilitated bilateral trade. In 1990, Sino–Japanese bilateral trade was of relatively small scale, amounting to US$18.1 billion. However, bilateral trade rose drastically — more than 19-fold — in the last two decades, hitting record high at US$345.9 billion in 2011. Despite a drop of about 13% in 2009 due to the global financial crisis, bilateral trade recovered quickly in the following year.

Following an export-oriented growth strategy, Japan had successfully achieved industrialisation and joined the club of high-income countries. It maintained the world's second-largest economy status for more than 40 years before being overtaken by China in 2010. Japan's post-World War II economic miracle can be attributed to international trade, which played a critical role. Its export-oriented development strategy further facilitated the development of its manufacturing industry, such as electronics, machinery and automobile, which became globally competitive and depended not only on domestic but also international markets. Therefore, the Japanese economy has not yet rebalanced itself towards domestic market despite its successful industrialisation. Even today as Japan's population continues to age and decline, exports remain an essential source of Japan's economic growth. China's transition from a closed to an open economy and unprecedented high growth in the last three decades had nurtured a new market of 1.4 billion population with a GDP per capita at over US$7,500, thereby providing enormous growth potential to Japanese exporting firms. Japanese firms' exports to China rose exponentially in the last two and half decades. In 1990, Japan exported US$6.1 billion worth of goods to China, about 2.1% of its total exports. China was then a relatively insignificant overseas market. As the Chinese economy continued to develop at double-digit growth rate, Japanese exports to China expanded drastically. By 2011, Japan's annual export volume to China surged more than 25 times vis-à-vis 1990 to US$162 billion, accounting for 19.7% of Japanese exports to the world (Figure 1). In 2004, for the first time, Japan's exports to China exceeded that to the United States. China has since become the largest market of Japanese exports, even though the Chinese economy remains less than two-thirds of the United States, the largest economy in the world.

China, similar to Japan, adopted an export-oriented growth strategy after it began its economic reform. Exports and savings accumulation from trade surplus were integral to China's development policy. Japan — a high-income country with a population of more than

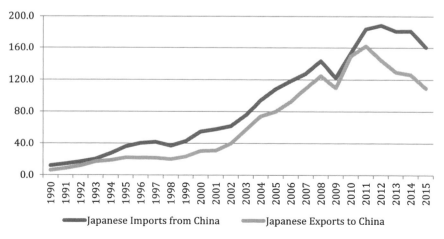

Figure 1. Bilateral Trade between China and Japan
Source: United Nations Comtrade Database.

125 million — has been an indispensable market of Chinese exports and also one of China's largest markets. In 1990, China's export to Japan was valued at US$12 billion. By 2012, as China continued to expand its exports to Japan, the annual volume hit a record high of US$188.5 billion, about 9.2% of China's total exports to the world. China also ran trade surplus with Japan every year between 1990 and 2015. The trade surplus per year increased substantially from US$5.9 billion to US$51.3 billion, contributing significantly to China's foreign exchange reserves.

It is noteworthy that more than half of China's exports to Japan belong to processing exports, which are manufactured with imported parts and components. Processing exports differ from ordinary exports in that the former are produced from substantial foreign value added content whereas all of the latter's value added are produced domestically. Processing exports have functioned as a vehicle for made-in-China products to enter the Japanese market. With abundant cheap labour, Chinese exports tend to be of relatively low cost. Low price is, however, just one of many factors determining competitiveness of products in international markets. Consumers of international markets, especially in high-income countries, prefer branded and high-tech products. It is therefore difficult for Chinese firms, which do not have globally recognised brands and intellectual proprietary right of high technology, to sell their products in international markets and compete with incumbent multinational firms. Processing exports, a subset of activities of global value chains (GVCs), are produced by assembling imported parts and components into ready-to-use final products. By participating in GVCs, Chinese firms are then able to sell their assembled products through global distribution networks established by lead firms of GVCs, thus leveraging the advantage of brands and advanced technologies owned by these lead firms. To a large extent, most of information communication and technology products exported by China, such as mobile phones, laptop computers, iPad and digital cameras, belong to the processing exports category and are assembled in China rather than made in China. Therefore, in addition to China's comparative advantage in labour endowment, GVCs have greatly

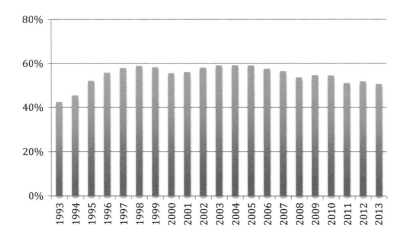

Figure 2. Share of Processing Exports in China's Exports to Japan

Source: Author's calculation based on data from General Administration of Customs of the People's Republic of China.

facilitated the penetration of Chinese exports to high-income countries, including Japan.[1]

In 1993, processing exports accounted for 43% of China's exports to Japan. As more multinational enterprises (MNEs), which utilised China as an export base, relocated their assembly capacities to China or outsourced low value-added tasks to Chinese firms, China's processing exports expanded rapidly and grew much faster than ordinary exports. Consequently, the share of processing exports in China's exports surged to 59% by 2005, suggesting that GVCs performed a vital role in facilitating growth of China's exports to Japan (Figure 2). Due to rising labour cost and the appreciation of the Chinese renminbi against the Japanese yen attributed to Japan's extraordinary monetary expansion, Chinese firms have gradually lost their competitiveness in low value-added task — i.e. assembly. The share of processing exports declined slightly in recent years, but still remained as high as 51% in

---

[1] Xing Yuqing, "Global Value Chains and China's Exports to High-income countries", *International Economic Journal*, vol. 30, no. 2, 2016, pp. 191–203.

2013 (Figure 2). A substantial portion of value added embedded in Chinese exports is produced by China's trading partners. In terms of processing exports, more than 50% of the value added was produced in foreign countries. For instance, about 77% of processing imports, the inputs necessary to produce processing exports, came from East Asian economies. Japan is among the top 10 sources of China's processing imports.[2] Therefore, China's trade surplus with Japan should be attributed to not only China but also to other countries, which sell parts and components to Chinese companies for manufacturing exports to Japan.

The growth momentum of the Sino–Japanese bilateral trade seemed to lose steam in recent years. Japan's imports from China decreased to US$160 billion in 2015, about 15% lower than in 2012. Japan's exports to China also decreased substantially to US$109 billion in 2015, about one-third of its peak in 2011 at US$162 billion. Several factors contributed to the contraction of bilateral trade. First, Japan's nationalisation of the Diaoyu/Senkaku islands triggered anti-Japanese demonstrations in China that had severely undermined the bilateral diplomatic relations, led to a deteriorating business environment, and higher risk of doing business. Second, many Japanese-affiliated firms in China utilised China as an export platform. They imported intermediate inputs from Japan and then used those imports to manufacture exports for Japanese markets. The activities of these firms contributed to increased bilateral trade. It was estimated that Japanese-affiliated manufacturing firms in China exported one-third of their products to Japan. Due to rising labour and land costs in China, many Japanese firms relocated their production facilities either back to Japan or third countries, thus resulting in a decrease in bilateral trade. Third, China's double-digit economic growth has ended. The demand of Chinese economy for Japanese products weakened following substantial economic slowdown since 2012. Without a doubt, compounded with almost zero growth, the shrinking aggregate demand of the Japanese

---

[2] Xing Yuqing, "Processing trade, Exchange Rates and China's Bilateral Trade Balances", *Journal of Asian Economics*, vol. 23, no. 5, 2012, pp. 540–547.

economy imposes additional constraints on China's exports to Japan, thereby hampering growth of bilateral trade too.

Japanese FDI in China: From Export to Domestic Oriented

Foreign direct investment is another channel of integrating Chinese and Japanese economy. Japan, holding about ¥340 trillion in net foreign assets, is one of the world's largest capital-exporting countries. Since the launch of its economic reform, the Chinese government has liberalised FDI by removing regulations that hindered foreign investment and by improving the legal environment of protecting foreign ownerships. In order to support foreign investors, the Chinese government adopted various preferential policies, such as income tax exemption, cheap industrial land supply, tariff exemption on the imports of intermediate inputs used for producing exports, etc. Encouraged by these attractive policies and a large pool of cheap labour, Japanese multinational firms flooded into China. If Hong Kong, China's No. 1 source of FDI, is excluded largely due to round tripping of domestic capital between mainland China and Hong Kong, Japan has been China's largest source of FDI. In 1995, Japanese MNEs invested US$3.2 billion in China. The annual inflows surged to US$13.5 billion in 2012, making China the No.1 host of Japanese FDI in Asia. According to Japan External Trade Organisation (JETRO), Japanese FDI stock in China totalled US$104 billion by the end of 2014, much larger than that from the United States, or any European countries.

Japan's direct investment in developing countries is traditionally export oriented. By relocating production capacities of mature industries to developing countries, Japanese MNEs strengthened their competitiveness by combining their edge in advanced technologies with the low production costs of developing countries. Kojima[3] referred Japanese FDI as "Japanese model" to differentiate it from that of

---

[3] Koyoshi Kojima, *Direct Foreign Investment: A Japanese Model of Multinational Business Operations*, London, Croom Helm, 1978.

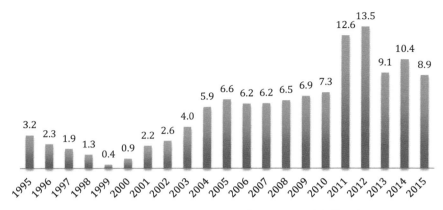

Figure 3. Japanese FDI in China (in US$ billion)
Source: Japan External Trade Organisation.

American and European MNEs. Low wage and abundant labour used to be decisive factors in attracting FDI. Most of Japanese FDI in China is export oriented.

Before 2005, most Japanese firms mainly utilised China as an export platform. The export orientation is evident in the structure of sale destinations of Japanese-affiliated manufacturers in China, which market their products not only locally but also abroad. In 1996, Japanese-affiliated manufacturers exported most of their products to overseas markets. The electrical machinery and transportation equipment sectors took up particularly large share of the exports. Japanese-affiliated manufacturers in the electrical machinery and transportation equipment sectors exported, respectively, 78% and 84% of their products (Figure 4). However, as Chinese economy grows and Chinese household income increases, Japanese-affiliated firms have gradually raised their sales in Chinese market, switching focus from overseas to the local market. The share of overseas markets thus decreased steadily while local sales rose rapidly. By 2005, the share of exports of Japanese-affiliated manufacturers as a whole decreased to 55%, and fell further to 31% in 2015. Japanese affiliates' operation in the transportation equipment sector experienced the most dramatic transition. In 2015, they exported only 6% of their products to overseas markets and sold

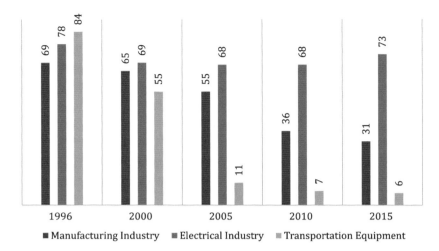

Figure 4. Export Intensity of Japanese-Affiliated Manufacturers in China
Source: Author's calculations based on data collected from Japan's Ministry of Finance.

the remaining 84% of products to Chinese consumers. Due to a sustained high growth, China has emerged as the largest automobile market in the world with annual sales of more than 20 million units. In addition, Chinese middle-class families regard automobiles as a standard and essential item. The strong growth of China's automobile market had fuelled Japanese affiliates' shift in market orientation from export to domestic market. Japanese affiliates' successful transition in their operation strategy demonstrates how foreign firms, which entered China for manufacturing exports at the early stage of China's development, could benefit in both the short and long run. In the short run, they could take advantage of the cheap labour while in the long run, benefit from a growing domestic market and rising Chinese household income since affordability of and demand for high-quality and big ticket items have increased. In electrical machinery sector, overseas markets still remain dominant. In 2015, Japanese affiliates exported 73% of their products to international markets but sold less than one-third in China's local market.

As it surpassed Japan to emerge as the world's second-largest economy, China has gradually lost its competitiveness in attracting export-oriented Japanese FDI. Rising wages and cumulative appreciation of the Chinese renminbi against the US dollar have greatly eroded China's comparative advantage in labour-intensive industry or labour-intensive tasks of GVCs. Some of the Japanese companies, which simply used China as a production base, had started to retreat. As a result, Japanese FDI inflows into China fell to US$9.1 billion in 2013, about 32.5% lower than in the preceding year. The FDI inflows recovered slightly in 2014 but slipped further to US$8.9 billion in 2015.

Besides economic factors, country risks, such as political instability in host countries and deteriorating diplomatic relations between FDI source countries and host countries, also play a determinant role in the location decision of MNEs' investment. In 2012, strong nationalist sentiments and subsequent violent anti-Japan protests in China broke the equilibrium of Sino–Japanese relations characterised by "hot economics, cold politics". Political tensions between the two countries had greatly exacerbated Japanese companies' perception of risks in China, and dampened their confidence of investing in the country. Political uncertainty and economic disincentives have driven many Japanese companies to actively adopt "China plus one" strategy, thus resulting in the fall of Japan's FDI in China.[4]

China's Mergers and Acquisitions in Japan

Foreign direct investment between China and Japan is no longer a one-way phenomenon. Chinese companies have begun their overseas expansion by investing abroad directly. Securing the supply of natural resources such as oil and minerals for the Chinese economy has motivated Chinese companies, especially state-owned enterprises, to invest massively in African and Latin American countries. With more than US$50 billion worth of completed deals, Chinese firms continue to be an important driver of global mergers and acquisitions (M&As). Energy and resources deals were a major driver of Chinese outbound

---

[4] Xing Yuqing, "Economic and Political Factors for the Fall of Japanese Foreign Direct Investment in China", *East Asian Policy*, vol. 8, no. 3, 2016, pp. 110–112.

M&A growth over the last decade, with US$30 billion spent on average each year between 2008 and 2013. M&As of financial services, real estate, technology and brands had grown rapidly in recent years.[5]

China's investment in Japan was purely driven by its hunger for strategic assets and intellectual property rights, such as advanced technology, globally recognised brands and international distributional networks. In terms of output, Chinese manufacturing industry currently ranks No. 1 in the world. However, Chinese firms lack globally recognised brands and competitive technologies. Most of them participate in low value-added segments of the GVCs — i.e. the assembly of parts and components into finished products. Participating in GVCs has enhanced Chinese companies' production capacity and increased their participation in the global market. To capture more value added, it is imperative for Chinese firms to move up the echelons of GVCs and become lead firms of GVCs. Many Chinese firms attempted to expand their sales in international markets but weak branding and global distribution networks were bottlenecks in their global expansion. To build strong global brands and develop global distribution networks from scratch require massive investment and are a long-term endeavour. Therefore, acquiring established companies with brand names and advanced technologies is a shortcut for firms of developing countries to catch up and compete with firms of developed countries in the global market.

Chinese M&A deals in Japan had exceeded US$1.0 billion in 2015, a 34% increase over the previous year. Compared with the United States, the scale of Chinese M&A in Japan remains relatively small. Nevertheless, those few high-profiled deals sealed by Chinese companies imply that Chinese investment in Japan is on an upward trend. Table 1 shows China's major M&As in Japan. In 2016, Midea, one of China's leading home appliance manufacturers, acquired an 80% stake in Toshiba Lifestyle Products & Services Corporation — the home appliances arm of Toshiba that manufactures and markets white goods, such as refrigerators, washing machines and vacuum cleaners. Toshiba's technology and

---

[5] Thilo Hanemann, *Chiba's Global Outbound M&A in 2014*, Rhodium Group, 2015.

Table 1. Major M&As by Chinese Companies

Year	Buyer	Target Company	Deal Size
2009	Suning Appliance	Laox	¥800 million for 27.36% shares
2010	Shangdong Ruyi	Renown	¥4 billion for 41% stake
2010	BYD	Ogihara	Unknown
2011	Haier	Sanyo Electric	¥10 billion
2016	Lenovo	NEC Lenovo Holding	US$195 million
2016	Midea	Toshiba Home Appliances	¥53.7 billion

Sources: Compiled from various news reports.

brand name are the prime target of the deal. Through this deal, Midea obtained the right to use the Toshiba brand worldwide in white goods business. Additionally, Midea received more than 5,000 intellectual property assets.[6] Another Chinese home appliance maker Haier made a similar deal in 2011 by acquiring Sanyo Electronic with ¥10 billion from Panasonic. The manufacturing facilities and distributors of Sanyo in Southeast Asia were transferred to Haier, thus significantly expanding Haier's distribution networks and visibility in the region. Sanyo's energy-efficient refrigerator technology and its "Aqua" brand were transferred to Haier, which uses and capitalises on "Aqua" brand to market refrigerators in both Japanese and overseas markets. In the face of stiff competition from Korean and Chinese electronics manufacturers, Japanese electronics companies gradually withdrew from home appliances industry. Chinese companies' M&As of Japanese electronics companies are win-win deals. On the one hand, Chinese companies acquired the technologies and brand names, which could strengthen Chinese companies' competitiveness and facilitate global expansion. On the other, Japanese sellers could use cash payment by Chinese buyers to improve balance sheets and carry out business restructuring. Another significant deal is the acquisition of NEC in a 44% stake by China's PC giant Lenovo in Lenovo–NEC joint venture for US$195 million. NEC introduced the

---

[6] Midea, "Toshiba and Midea Agree on the Transfer of Toshiba's Home Appliances", press release, 2016.

first PC in Japan in the late 1970s. It is currently the No. 1 PC maker with a market share of about 20% in Japan — the world's third-largest PC market. Lenovo had struggled to penetrate the Japanese market, even after acquiring IBM's PC business. In 2011, Lenovo and NEC hence set up a joint venture. Lenovo expected to take advantage of NEC's solid foothold in Japan, such as NEC's contract portfolio with large local companies and government agencies to expand its market share. After five years of cooperation, the joint venture propelled Lenovo to become the largest PC maker in Japan. The deal will further strengthen Lenovo's status as leading PC producer in the global market and support the growth of its core business.

In short, Midea's and Haier's acquisitions target three properties: brand names, technologies and distribution networks of Japanese firms. Lenovo's deal, on the other hand, targeted at NEC's well-established domestic distribution channel and its PC laboratory. There are also some Chinese companies that primarily concentrate on technology of targeted Japanese firms. For example, BYD, China's leading electric carmaker, took over a factory from Ogihara Corp., a major Japanese metal die manufacturer, to produce high-precision metal dies for its Chinese factories. Dies made with higher precision can in fact improve the quality of auto bodies and other products. This acquisition hence helped BYD narrow the technology gap with its Japanese and Western rivals.

Challenged by an ageing and declining population, many Japanese companies have been struggling with survival in the domestic market. They do have the capacity to expand overseas on their own. Chinese M&As have offered financially distressed Japanese companies access to China's market, which has a fast-growing middle class. Shandong Ruyi's acquisition of Japanese apparel maker Renown Inc. is a typical example. Renown is one of Japan's best-known clothes makers with more than 100 years of history. The president of Renown commented that the tie-up with Shandong Ruyi would boost the struggling company's capital and facilitate its overseas expansion, particularly in fast-growing China.[7] Shandong Ruyi could also capitalise on Renown's quality

---

[7] M Nakamoto, "China's Ruyi to Pay Y4bn for Renown", *The Financial Time*, 25 May 2010.

control, manufacturing know-how and Renown's famous brand D'urban, which is already well regarded by affluent Chinese consumers.

Chinese Tourist Arrivals in Japan

China's improved economic integration with Japan can also be discerned from the tide of Chinese tourists into Japan. China has now become the largest source of foreign tourists to Japan. In 2015, nearly five million Chinese visited Japan, accounting for a quarter of foreign visitors to Japan. Such "explosive growth" of Chinese tourists occurred in recent years. In 2013, 1.3 million Chinese visited Japan. The number surged to 2.4 million in 2014, a growth of more than 80%. In 2015, Chinese tourist arrivals in Japan further jumped to five million, doubling that in 2014 (Figure 5). Why do Chinese tourists suddenly love Japan?

There is no lack of ill will in China towards Japan. The chilly diplomatic relationship between China and Japan is matched by occasional expressions of antagonism by the Chinese public. The 2016 Genron NPO survey reveals that 76.7% of surveyed Chinese had "negative impression" of Japan. Even though the proportion of surveyed Chinese

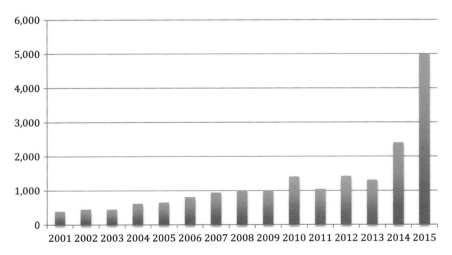

Figure 5. Chinese Tourist Arrivals in Japan (in thousands)

Source: Japan Tourism Agency.

who viewed Japan negatively decreased substantially, by comparison to the 2013 survey conducted just after Japan's nationalisation of the Diaoyu/Senkaku Islands, the survey suggests that majority of Chinese had an unfavourable opinion of Japan. Despite the apparent disdain, Chinese tourists place Japan top on their overseas travel destinations list, a reflection of how Chinese holidaymakers are immune to deteriorating diplomatic relations.

Weak Japanese yen, Japan's relaxation of visa requirement, and China's high tariffs and non-tariff barriers imposed on foreign consumer goods are some of the reasons that explain the flood of Chinese visitors to Japan. Abenomics' "first arrow" of quantitative easing had induced sharp depreciation of Japanese yen against Chinese renminbi, from ¥100 yen for RMB8.3 to ¥100 for RMB5.0. From Chinese tourists' perspective, the Japanese yen depreciation means an automatic discount of 40% on prices of all services and goods sold in Japanese domestic market. Chinese tourists often schedule shopping sprees when they are outside of the country. The sharp discount therefore made Japan an attractive shopping haven. Moreover, preferences of Chinese consumers, particularly the middle-income families, have evolved from chasing cheap products to coveting high-quality products. "Made in Japan" products are well known for their high quality among Chinese consumers. In China's domestic market, products labelled with Japanese brands are made in China rather than in Japan. Hence, travelling to Japan offers the opportunity to purchase high-quality "Made in Japan" products. In fact, daily necessities, such as cosmetics, traditional Chinese medicine, rice cookers, baby formula, diapers, etc., make up bulk of Chinese tourists' shopping list.

According to Japan Tourism Agency,[8] Chinese tourists' expenditure accounted for 46.6% of total foreign tourist spending in Japan. On average, a Chinese tourist in Japan spent ¥280,000, more than 50% higher than the average spending of all foreign visitors to Japan. Each Chinese tourist spent ¥140,000 in shopping on average, almost

---

[8] Japan Tourism Agency, "Survey of Foreign Tourist Spending: July–September 2015", 2015.

doubled the average shopping expenditure of all foreign visitors to Japan. The flood of Chinese tourists had indeed greatly alleviated the pain of Japanese retail and service industries, which have suffered from shrinking domestic demand. Due to the surge in Chinese tourist arrivals, Tokyo and other major metropolitan cities are facing hotel accommodation shortage, which is good news to Japan's real estate sector. Abenomics' "third arrow" focuses on structural reforms. The promotion of tourism to stimulate domestic consumption is actually one of the agenda in Japan's structural reforms. The Abe administration had aimed to increase the number of foreign visitors to 20 million by 2020. Thanks to Chinese visitors, the target was achieved five year earlier.

Concluding Remarks

The Sino–Japanese economic integration has evolved into a new stage. Apart from the massive bilateral trade and Japanese FDI worth more than US$100 billion in China, Chinese companies have also started to target Japanese companies in their acquisition of brand names, technology and global distribution networks, which are indispensable assets for Chinese companies to strengthen their competitiveness and move up to high value-added echelons of GVCs. Chinese M&As in Japan also enhance the access of target Japanese companies to China's huge market and improve their balance sheets. The flood of Chinese tourists into Japan had boosted Japan's retail sales and the demand for other services such as hotels and restaurants. Increased economic integration between China and Japan obviously enhanced the welfare of both countries.

Despite China's high economic growth for more than three decades, Chinese companies are far from being competent competitors of Japanese companies in many areas. Japan's and China's economic structures are largely complementary rather than competitive. Further integration between the two will surely create tremendous economic benefits. Geopolitical concerns and the Senkaku/Diaoyu Islands territorial dispute have stalled the establishment of institutional relations for enhancing bilateral economic cooperation, thereby leaving market forces as the sole driver of Sino–Japanese economic integration.

Chapter 9

The Political Economy of East Asia Economic Integration

John WONG & KONG Tuan Yuen*

East Asia (EA) is, geographically speaking, made up of Northeast Asia (China, Japan and Korea) and Southeast Asia (the 10 ASEAN countries). Politically, this constitutes the ASEAN plus Three or APT. Economically, EA as an economic region in the past referred to Japan, China the newly industrialised economies (NIEs) of Korea, Taiwan, Hong Kong and Singapore, and the ASEAN-4 of Indonesia, Malaysia, the Philippines and Thailand.

Most of the EA economies were historically high-performance economies, having achieved dynamic growth for a sustained period. EA growth was commonly generated by high investment and high savings. It was also based on exported-oriented development strategies. Institutionally, EA growth has been generally supported by pro-growth and pro-market active government intervention — the so-called "Developmental State" model.

---

* John WONG was Professorial Fellow at the East Asian Institute, National University of Singapore. KONG Tuan Yuen is Visiting Research Fellow at the same institute.

The first wave of EA's high growth was led by Japan in the 1960s, the 1970s and much of the 1980s; and it soon spread to the four NIEs and some ASEAN economies. This marks the first rise of EA or EA-I. Japanese economists used to explain such a phenomenon as the "flying geese pattern". The second wave of EA's high growth was led by China, which chalked up even more impressive growth since its economic reform in 1979. China's growth is currently spreading to the whole of the EA region.

Such is the second rise of EA or EA-II, which is economically much more formidable than EA-I, because of China's vast economic scale compounded by its high growth rates. The China-led EA-II as of 2013 accounted for 24.4% of global GDP (higher than the US share of 21.5%), as compared to 15.2% of the Japan-led EA-I. Increasingly, China's economy operates not just as an engine of growth for the EA region, but also a catalyst for regional economic integration.

After the 2008 global financial crisis, global economic gravity had clearly shifted to EA. However, individual EA economies are still beset by problems of structural imbalance. Above all, the future of EA-II still critically depends on the continuing economic rise of China, namely, the ability of China's economy to sustain its dynamic economic growth without falling into the "middle-income trap".

China's double-digit hyper growth has just come to an end and its future growth depends much on its further economic reform and success in its macroeconomic rebalancing as well as cultivating of new sources of growth, for example, higher productivity and greater technological progress. Japan in the meantime is taking strong measures to revive its stagnant economy while the other EA economies are also adjusting themselves to the "New Normal" of China's slower economic growth.

The existing regional economic order in EA will, therefore, continue to be marred by uncertainty and instability. It is still a long way from the East Asian Community, which is to be based on not just sustainable economic growth and increasing integration, but also harmonious political and security relations.

The Growth of East Asia

In the contemporary history of Asia's economic development, Japan was unquestionably the first successfully industrialised economy to be able to compete with the advanced Western countries. Japan led the first rise of East Asia's growth (EA-I) and reached high economic growth in the 1950s and 1960s and became the second largest economy in the world in the middle of the 1970s. In 1975, Japan had also succeeded in enrolling in the exclusive Group of Seven (G7).

Regionally, the successful industrialisation of Japan has in turn spread to other Asian newly industrialised economies. Japanese economists called this "Flying Geese" or FG pattern, based on the theory of "shifting comparative advantage" to address the catching-up process of industrialisation in developing economies.[1] Originally, the concept of FG pattern came from Kaname Akamatsu's Japanese articles in 1930s which was later introduced to the western world in the beginning of the 1960s in English. Subsequently, the concept was expanded to describe the path of industry's international transmission like flying geese, from a lead goose (Japan) to follower geese (NIEs, ASEAN 4, China and so on).

EA-I was widely recognised in terms of FG development in the 1980s when Okita Saburo, the Japanese economist and former foreign minister, gave a famous speech on FG development at the fourth Pacific Economic Cooperation Council conference held in Seoul in 1985. Okita explained that Japan used to be a follower in the late 19th century to catch-up with the development of advanced western countries by manufacturing nondurable consumer goods at first, then durable consumer goods and involved in capital goods. The Asian NIEs and the ASEAN countries had undergone the experience of Japan in FG development by supportive of the division of labour.[2] The regional transmission of

---

[1] K Akamatsu, "Historical Pattern of Economic Growth in Developing Countries", *The Developing Economies*, vol. 1, 1962, pp. 3–25. K Kojima, "The 'Flying Geese' Model of Asian Economic Development: Origin, Theoretical Extensions, and Regional Policy Implications", *Journal of Asian Economics*, vol. 11, 2000, pp. 375–401.

[2] Okita S, "Special Presentation: Prospect of Pacific Economies". Korea Development Institute, "Pacific Cooperation: Issues and Opportunities", Report of the Fourth Pacific Economic Cooperation Conference, Seoul, Korea, 29 April through 1 May 1985, pp. 18–29.

FG development has been supported by the "pro-trade oriented FDI" policy by investing in the country's comparatively disadvantageous production. Japan as the region's dominant economy provided an important source of growth for other EA economies by supplying capital (FDI), technology and market. This facilitated the development of the NIEs and other latecomers while simultaneously enhancing EA economic integration by trade and investment.

The Japanese economy slowed down when the Japanese asset price bubble burst in the late of the 1990s. It quickly influenced NIEs and ASEAN countries in terms of investment. At the time, China had gradually taken part of the economic leadership in the region to lead the second wave of EA growth or EA-II.

In the last three decades, China has enjoyed dynamic growth since 1978 and created average growth of 9.8% from 1979 to 2013. China's hyper-growth period was historically much longer than that of the NIEs for which Japan and Korea had just experienced about two decades of growth while Singapore's and Hong Kong's were much shorter. As a latecomer of Asia's growth, China has not only internationally taken advantage of technological accumulation from advanced economies such as Japan, but also locally enjoyed its "demographic dividend", the larger labour force, with much bigger hinterland.[3] Meanwhile, China experienced low inflation for most years, especially after the 1998 financial crisis.

Based on the continuously good performance on economic growth, China has risen from regional to global economic power at the beginning of the 21st century. In the data of World Bank in 2015, China's nominal gross domestic product (GDP) was about US$10.9 trillion, the world's number two economy led by the United States (about US$17.9 trillion) and the European Union (about US$16.2 trillion), but number one in GDP in terms of purchasing power parity, about US$19.5 trillion.[4]

---

[3] John Wong, "China's Economy 2014/15: Adjusting to the "New Normal" of Moderate Growth", *EAI Background Brief*, no. 980, East Asian Institute, National University of Singapore, 2014, p. 3.
[4] The World Bank, World Development Indicators, available at <http://data.worldbank.org/data-catalog/world-development-indicators> (accessed 8 December 2016).

China's growth was mostly attributed to the rapid trade expansion. Total trade grew 15% for the period of 1979–2012. China has also become the world's largest exporting country since 2009 and the largest trading nation registering over US$4 trillion in trade in 2013. Most importantly, more than half of China's trade flows to the Asian region for the last two decades and major trading partners of EA countries, which included Japan, NIEs and ASEAN4, at least accounted for one third of the yearly total trade (Figure 1). It showed that China's trade expansion has persistent effect on EA countries and contributed to the regional economic integration.

Overall, EA is a natural and compact economic region made up of fairly complementary components. Japan as the most developed country in the region was economically well complemented by the four NIEs and the resource-rich ASEAN economies while the four manufactured-based NIEs are also in complementarity with the resource-rich ASEAN. China, vast and diverse, adds new impetus and new sources to the region's growth and integration. China not only operates a new engine of economic growth for the other EA economies but also a catalyst for regional economic integration. It is home to numerous regional and global production networks. Obviously, EA-II is more formidable than the previous wave.

East Asia Economic Integration

Economic integration is always related to the process of abolishing discrimination among the economy under particular economic institution, for example the Free Trade Agreement (FTA). It is commonly defined as an agreement among countries to remove trade barriers in order to promote free trade and investment for greater economic efficiency and hence higher GDP growth by "trade creation" and "trade diversion" effects.[5] Economic integration has several forms, including

---

[5] R T Dalimov, "The Dynamics of the Trade Creation and Diversion Effects Under International Economic Integration", *Current Research Journal of Economic Theory*, 2009, vol. 1, issue 1.

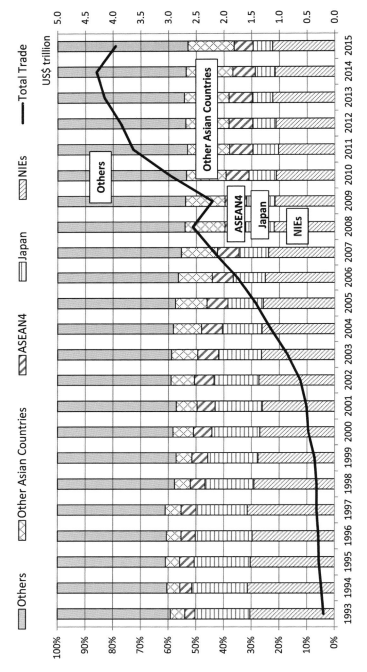

Figure 1. China's Trade: Total by Country Grouping 1993–2015

Source: CEIC Data Manager.

free trade agreement, custom union, common market, economic union and complete economic integration.[6]

The hierarchy of economic integration can be considered as the level of abolishing economic discrimination. Generally, FTA focuses on the elimination of tariff and non-tariff regulation in trade for members while retaining tariffs for nonmembers. Custom union generalises the member's tariff in commodity movement with nonmembers, while common market moves further to remove the restriction of factor movement and economic union combines custom union and common market to coordinate with members' own national economic policy. In complete economic integration, members are willing to abandon their own economic policy, especially the monetary and fiscal policies, to follow the decision of supranational authority.

In reality, it is nothing but the FTA that is often promoted and implemented around the world. Among the FTAs, the Regional Trade Agreements are relatively well-developed and increasing in numbers after the period of Cold War. For example, ASEAN Free Trade Area (1993), North American Free Trade Agreement (1994), Commonwealth of Independent States (1994), ASEAN-China (2005 in goods and 2007 in services) and most of the enlargement of European Commission are in force since 1991. By the records of World Trade Organisation, there are over 600 regional trade agreements (Figure 2) globally while there are about 100 in East Asia, albeit with only 24 in operation.

The role of ASEAN has become crucial because it is the only formal and rules-based regional organisation in the EA region. Though ASEAN has existed for almost 50 years, it was formed in 1967 by only five founding members. Brunei joined in 1984, and Cambodia, Lao PDR, Myanmar and Vietnam in the 1990s. ASEAN is today often hailed as one of most successful regional groupings in the developing world. Arguably also the longest-lasting regional organisation, ASEAN's continued existence is in reality unique, as virtually all past Third World regional groupings either collapsed or became defunct.

---

[6] Bela Balassa, *The Theory of Economic Integration*, Routledge Revivals, Routledge, 2013, p. 2.

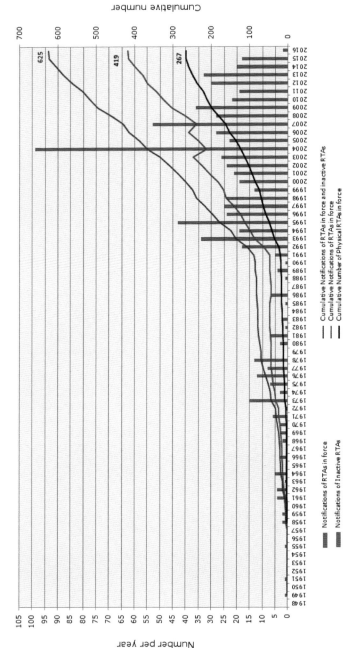

Figure 2. Evolution of Regional Trade Agreements in the World, 1948–2016[7]

Note: Notification of RTAs: good, services and accessions to an RTA are counted separately. Physical RTAs: good, and accessions to an RTA are counted together.

Source: WTO Secretariat.

---

[7] The figure has been retrieved from WTO Secretariat, available at <https://www.wto.org/english/tratop_e/region_e/regfac_e.htm> (accessed 18 January 2017).

Table 1. Intra-regional Trade Share: Selected Years (%)

	1990	1995	2000	2005	2010	2015
ASEAN	17.0	21.1	22.7	24.9	24.6	23.7
CJK	12.3	18.6	20.3	23.7	22.1	19.5
RCEP	33.0	40.4	40.6	43.1	44.2	43.4
TPP	40.0	44.3	48.1	43.5	39.0	40.1
APEC	67.7	71.8	72.5	69.6	67.5	69.4

Note: CJK refers to China, Japan and Korea; RCEP refers to Regional Comprehensive Economic Partnership; TPP refers to Trans-Pacific Partnership; and APEC refers to Asia-Pacific Economic Cooperation.

Source: The Direction of Trade Statistics, IMF.

The first round of economic cooperation based on trade liberation, ASEAN's joint industrial projects and ASEAN's industrial complementation schemes did not work out well. Its progress towards regional economic integration was slow; intra-ASEAN trade was around 20% during ASEAN's first two decades. In 2010s, it only increased to around 24-25% (Table 1 and Figure 3) partly because most ASEAN economies are externally integrated, namely, with non-ASEAN states. However, ASEAN has made efforts towards achieving the ASEAN Economic Community and becoming a single market by the end of 2015.

Compared with intra-regional trade, ASEAN has been conspicuously much more successful in its "extra-regional cooperation", such as extending political and economic linkages to other countries and providing a variety of multilateral frameworks for a wide range of extra-regional cooperation activities, including various Track I, II and III cooperation mechanisms. Strategically, ASEAN is indeed well-located for all sorts of cooperation activities while politically ASEAN offers a good buffer for contending powers both within the region and without.

Through the ASEAN post-ministerial conference mechanisms, Australia, Canada, China, EU, India, Japan, Korea and USA become ASEAN's economic dialogue partners especially the ASEAN plus three

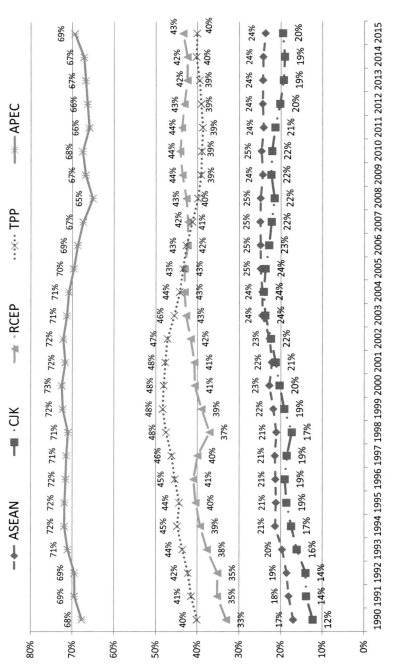

Figure 3. Intra-regional Trade Share: 1990–2015 (%)

Source: The Direction of Trade Statistics, IMF.

(APT or 10+3) which comprise all 10 ASEAN countries, China, Japan and Korea. APT further broadens ASEAN's cooperation into EA as a whole including East Asia Summit, APT plus three (APT plus India, Australia and New Zealand or 10+3+3) and APT plus three plus two (APT plus three plus United States and Russia or 10+3+2).

Politically, ASEAN Regional Forum as a multilateral framework contributes to peaceful conflict resolution in the region and stable security architecture. ARF was established in 1994 to build constructive dialogue and consultation on political and security issues and to implement significant confidence-building and preventive diplomacy in the Asia-Pacific region. Participants in ARF are from a wider area than that of economic dialogue partners which include Australia, Bangladesh, Brunei Darussalam, Cambodia, Canada, China, Democratic People's Republic of Korea, European Union, India, Indonesia, Japan, Lao PDR, Malaysia, Mongolia, Myanmar, New Zealand, Pakistan, Papua New Guinea, Philippines, Republic of Korea, Russia, Singapore, Sri Lanka, Thailand, Timor-Leste, United States and Vietnam.

Significantly, ASEAN now stands to gain from its wide-ranging extra-regional cooperation activities, without incurring much adjustment costs. Accordingly, ASEAN today has become a highly visible regional grouping, with a lot of political clout.

Regional Comprehensive Economic Partnership, Trans-Pacific Partnership and Free Trade Area of the Asia Pacific

EA is currently a pivot to three mega-FTA schemes: The Regional Comprehensive Economic Partnership (RCEP), Trans-Pacific Partnership (TPP) and Free Trade Area of the Asia Pacific (FTAAP). Some EA countries are included in all these mega-FTA schemes, for example Japan, while others take part in one or two (Figure 4).

RCEP makes up of 16 countries, which is literally APT plus three. It was launched during the EAS (East Asia Summit) in Phnom Penh in November 2012 by leaders of 16 countries. The objectives of RCEP are

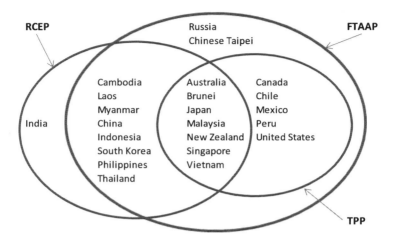

Figure 4. Mega-FTA Schemes in Asia and Trans-Pacific Region
Source: Compiled by authors.

to reach a "modern, comprehensive, high-quality and mutually beneficial economic partnership agreement" aimed at establishing an open trade and investment environment in the region to facilitate expansion of regional trade and investment and contribute to global and regional economic growth. It has gone through more than 20 rounds of negotiation and is likely to come to conclude by end 2018.[8] RCEP is potentially one of the world's largest FTA groupings, accounting for one third of global GDP and one half of the world's population.[9]

ASEAN has been the cornerstone in the evolution of the RCEP process. ASEAN owed its survival and continuing existence to its special techniques of organising regional cooperation, commonly known as the "ASEAN Way" or the "Southeast Asian Way". Therefore, the "ASEAN Way" of conducting regional cooperation based on more

---

[8] "Conclusion for Regional Comprehensive Economic Partnership 'Finally in Sight': PM Lee", available at <https://www.channelnewsasia.com/news/singapore/asean-regional-comprehensive-economic-partnership-pm-lee-10662722> (accessed 30 August 2018).

[9] "Asia Advances RCEP Talks as Trump's Trade Policy Unites Members", *Nikkei Asian Review*, 31 August 2018. Availabe at <https://asia.nikkei.com/Economy/Asia-advances-RCEP-talks-as-Trump-s-trade-policy-unites-members> (accessed 1 October 2018).

consultation and building consensus may be a useful reference to RCEP. However, China, being the largest economy in the group, is certainly the most crucial for driving the integration of RCEP.

TPP is an even more ambitious FTA grouping, covering two thirds of global GDP and one third of global trade. It is aiming to develop into a high-quality FTA, including measures to address sensitive issues like intellectual property rights, state-owned enterprises and labour protection. TPP currently makes up of 11 member countries, also known as the Comprehensive and Progressive Agreement for Trans-Pacific Partnership (CPTPP) including Australia, Brunei, Canada, Chile, Japan, Malaysia, Mexico, New Zealand, Peru, Singapore and Vietnam, after the withdrawal of the United States.

There are four ASEAN countries taking part in TPP negotiation. Singapore, already very open but still pushing TPP, may gain much direct benefits in the short run. Vietnam expects to gain a lot more for having greater access to members' market for its labour-intensive exports and its state-owned enterprise reform will step up. Malaysia's Malay-based state-owned enterprises may face problems. Japan also expects to gain due to de-regulation and further reform and liberalisation.

TPP had been supported by the US Senate and all participants in TPP had already succeeded to reach an agreement by the end of 2015. Unfortunately, Donald John Trump, the new US president, has not supported its ratification. Trump had quit TPP trade deal on the first day he took office. Trump looked upon TPP as "a potential disaster for our country" and turn to "negotiate fair bilateral trade deals that bring jobs and industry back".

From 2006, Asia-Pacific Economic Cooperation (APEC) leaders have issued "Pathway to FTAAP" to study FTAAP which include all 21 APEC members' economic integration. By the 22nd APEC summit held in Beijing in November 2014, the Annex A of the leaders' declaration, named "Beijing Roadmap for APEC's Contribution to the Realisation of the FTAAP" was publicised to further pave the concrete steps.

President Xi Jinping had again advocated FTAAP at the 24th APEC meeting in November 2016. Xi urged APEC economies to promote an open and integrated economy by pushing forward connectivity to achieve joint development, boosting innovation to create internal driving force and promoting mutual beneficial cooperation to strengthen strong partnership. The "Annex A: Lima Declaration on FTAAP" was announced to complete and enhance the possible pathways for the realisation of FTAAP, continue APEC's role as an incubator to support FTAAP, implement new initiatives to advance regional economic integration and strengthen consultation with stakeholders.

Compared with other members of ASEAN, Singapore is the most developed and industrialised economy. Singapore is also the most open economy for foreign trade and foreign investment. Based on the Index of Economic Freedom, Singapore is the second freest economy in the world for the 22nd consecutive year, just behind Hong Kong; hence Singapore has all along stood for free trade.

Singapore has been a strong supporter of ASEAN's economic cooperation initiatives and has also actively participated in ASEAN + 3 and ASEAN + 6 regional cooperation initiatives. Singapore currently has 21 FTAs and Economic Partnership Agreements in operation, with 32 trading partners, including ASEAN FTA partners.

Singapore has been highly active in taking part in regional economic integration. Singapore is both members of RCEP and TPP and one of the four original founding members of the TPP. Most RCEP and TPP members are already Singapore's top trade partners. In 2015, the trade percentage of Singapore with TPP members was 46.6%, with RCEP members was 62.1% and with APEC members was 75.6%.[10] Singapore believes that both TPP and RCEP are mutually reinforcing parallel tracks to deepen regional integration and two complementary building blocs to enhance trade and FDI flows to both Singapore and the region. Most importantly, both aim at the long-term objective of FTAAP.

Concluding Remarks

The TPP holds great promises to become the world's most formidable FTA grouping in future, even though the United States has currently

---

[10] The figures are calculated by authors from the Direction of Trade Statistics, IMF.

withdrawn from it under the Trump administration. One of its potential problems is that TPP has become too politicised. For this reason, China, despite being the largest trading power, is conspicuously excluded from the pact. As China is home to numerous regional and global production networks, its exclusion could affect the trade pattern of the TPP.

In fact, RCEP and TPP are created as two separate trade blocs to complement rather than compete with each other, as some members of RCEP are also members of TPP. In this sense, both can be seen as mutually reinforcing parallel tracks to deepen regional economic integration. In the long run, both aim at the long-term objective of reaching the same areas as the FTAAP — when the geo-political landscape of the region in future is no longer at odds with its geo-economic arrangements. The future challenge is the convergence between RECP and TPP. ASEAN can provide a useful foundation for the FTA endeavour. ASEAN is strategically well-located and politically a good buffer for contending powers.

If politics from all sides is working well, FTAAP could become an umbrella FTA grouping for the whole region. Ideally, it is also an opportunity to incorporate RCEP with TPP into FTAAP. However, trade and politics are inseparable. All the processes including trade negotiation and implementation, and adjustment to free trade, are political because there are uneven distribution of benefits and costs in the initial phase. More incredibly, the anti-trade and anti-globalisation sentiments in industrial democracies currently threaten global economic integration.

Index

21st-Century Maritime Silk Road, 104, 118

Abenomics, 148–149
appreciation of the Chinese renminbi, 138, 143
ASEAN, 4–5, 81, 103–115, 117–118, 134, 151, 153–155, 157, 159–164
    Plus One, 28, 81
    Plus Three (APT), 29, 151, 159, 161
ASEAN Economic Community, 159
ASEAN Regional Forum (ARF), 161
Asian Infrastructure Investment Bank (AIIB), 27, 81, 104, 118
Asia-Pacific Economic Cooperation (APEC), 81, 159–160, 163–164
Asian Paradox, 119

Belt and Road Initiative, 3–4, 27, 50, 100–101
bilateral trade, 5, 10, 68, 72, 81–82, 104–109, 111–112, 122, 125, 134–135, 139–140, 149, 163
    China–ASEAN, 105–107
    development, 68, 72
    Sino–Japanese, 134–136, 139
bonds market, 34–35, 41, 43
business models of Chinese enterprises, 59

capital account, 33–35, 38–40, 43, 49
    liberalisation, 35, 38–39, 49
CEPA-induced business receipts, 95
CEPA-induced export of services, 95
China's investment
    in Cambodia, Laos, Myanmar and Vietnam, 115
    in Japan, 144
    in Korea, 124
    in Taiwan, 75
China–ASEAN bilateral trade, 105–107
China–ASEAN economic relations, 103–105, 117–118

167

China–ASEAN Free Trade Area (CAFTA), 103–104
China–ASEAN FTA, 29–31, 81
China–ASEAN trade, 109
China–Japan–Korea (CJK) trilateral summit, 121–122, 130–131
China–South Korea agreement, 31
China–South Korea FTA, 29–31, 81
Chinese Communist Party (CCP), the, 70, 130
CJK meeting, 132
Closer Economic Partnership Agreement (CEPA), 85–92, 95–98, 100
Comprehensive and Progressive Agreement for Trans-Pacific Partnership (CPTPP), 163
cross-strait
    economic relations, 4, 68, 82
    economic integration, 80
    relations, 76,
currency internationalisation, 33

Democratic Progressive Party (DPP), the, 68, 79
Diaoyu/Senkaku islands, 139, 148–149
diplomatic rift, 121, 125
direct investment, 1, 5, 13–14, 98, 104, 112–113, 115–117, 140
    inward foreign, 1
    foreign (FDI), 13, 39, 52–53, 68, 99, 112, 123–124, 134, 140, 143
    outward, 3, 18, 104, 115–116

East Asia Summit, 161
East Asian economies, 1–2, 7–8, 10, 14, 16, 18, 22, 139
Economic Cooperation Framework Agreement (ECFA), 68, 71, 75, 77–78, 83
economic integration
    East Asian, 3, 5, 7
    interregional, 117
    regional, 4, 81, 83, 100, 120–122, 127, 152, 155, 159, 164–165
economic interaction, 96–97, 106
    Hong Kong–Mainland, 96–97
exchange rate regime, 35, 38, 49
    renminbi, 35
export-oriented growth strategy, 135–136

Factory Asia, 7, 21
flying geese, 5, 7, 152–153
    model, 5, 7
    pattern, 152–153
foreign direct investment (FDI), 1, 13–15, 19, 39, 52–53, 57, 64–65, 68, 75, 82, 99, 112–116, 123–124, 134, 140–141, 143, 149, 154, 164
Free Trade Area of the Asia Pacific (FTAAP), 81, 161–165
free trade agreement(s) (FTAs), 28–29, 77–78, 80–81, 83, 85, 88, 115, 133, 155, 157, 164
    ASEAN, 30
    China–ASEAN, 29–30, 81
    China–South Korea, 29–30, 81
    South Korea–China, 125

global supply chain(s), 2, 108
global value chains (GVCs),
    137–138, 143–144, 149
globalisation, 7, 47, 52, 65
    economic, 3, 7

information and communications
    technology (ICT), 20, 69
    components, 73
    products, 73
    sectors, 69, 73
intellectual property rights, 144,
    163
International Monetary Fund
    (IMF), 3, 34, 38, 42–49
internationalisation
    of China's currency, 33, 56
    of Chinese enterprises, 51
    renminbi (RMB), 3, 33–35,
        38–41, 43, 49–50
intra-regional trade, 5, 159–160
investment facilitation, 3, 29, 86

Kuomintang (KMT), the, 67,
    70

Ma Ying-jeou, 69, 80
manufacturing exports, 139, 142
mergers and acquisitions (M&As),
    5, 61–62, 143–146, 149
monetary expansion, 138

New Southward Policy, 79
newly industrialised economics
    (NIEs), 151–156
Northeast Asia, 121
    regional economic integration
        of, 120

offshore processing, 60
outbound mergers and acquisitions
    (M&As), 61–62, 64, 143
outward foreign direct investment
    (OFDI), 14, 18–20, 53–54,
    56–58, 112–113

perpetual peace, 119
processing exports, 10, 137–139
processing imports, 139
production network(s), 5, 20, 72,
    155
    East Asian, 3, 7–8, 16, 21
    regional, 2, 7, 17, 106, 108,
        155

Regional Comprehensive Economic
    Partnership (RCEP), 5, 28–29,
    81, 134, 159–165
regional integration, 119, 127,
    164
renminbi
    exchange rate, 34
    exchange rate regime, 35
    internationalisation, 33–35,
        38–41, 43, 49–50
round-tripping, 57

services trade, 77, 97, 100
Silk Road Fund, the, 4, 104, 118
Sino–Japanese bilateral trade,
    134–135, 139
Sino–Japanese economic
    integration, 149
Sino–Korean bilateral relationship,
    120, 122
Sino–Korean economic relations,
    122

special drawing rights (SDR) basket, 34–35, 42–48
stock connect scheme(s), 34, 39–41
super-sovereign reserve money, 47–48
SWIFT (the society for Worldwide Interbank Financial Telecommunication), 40, 45

Taiwan's investment in China, 68–69, 71, 76

Terminal High Altitude Area Defence (THAAD), 5, 121, 125, 129–131
trade liberalisation, 82, 86, 135
Trans-Pacific Partnership (TPP), 28, 30–31, 159–165
Tsai Ing-wen, 4, 68, 78–80, 83–84

World Trade Organisation (WTO), the, 51–52, 69, 81, 96, 103, 105, 134–135, 157–158